Tipbook
Music on Paper
Basic Theory

Hugo Pinksterboer and Bart Noorman

Tipbook
Music on
Paper *Basic Theory*

HAL•LEONARD®

The Complete Guide to Your Instrument!

First edition published in 2002 by
The Tipbook Company bv, The Netherlands

Third edition published in 2010 by
Hal Leonard Books
An Imprint of Hal Leonard Corporation
7777 West Bluemound Road
Milwaukee, WI 53213

Trade Book Division Editorial Offices
33 Plymouth Street
Montclair, NJ 07042

Printed in the United States of America

Book design by Gijs Bierenbroodspot

Library of Congress Cataloging-in-Publication Data

Pinksterboer, Hugo.
  Tipbook music on paper / Hugo Pinksterboer. -- 2nd ed.
      p. cm. — (Tipbook series)
  "First edition published in 2002 by The Tipbook Company bv, The Netherlands."
  Includes bibliographical references and index.
  ISBN 978-1-4234-6529-4 (pbk.)
  1. Musical notation. 2. Music theory--Elementary works. I. Title.
      II. Title: Music on paper. III. Series.
  MT35.P65 2010
  781.4'23—dc22
                                        2010045125

Thanks!

Many thanks go to trumpeter and conservatory teacher Bart Noorman, who supplied a great deal of the information gathered in this book. Do check out his Virtual Music School at www.virtualmusicschool.org! Duncan Clark, thank you for your valuable additions.

For their information, their expertise, their time, and their help we'd also like to thank the following musicians, teachers, and other experts: Steve Clover, Elliot Freedman, Charli Green, Gerard Braun, Davina Cowan, Theo Olof, John van der Veer, Jeroen Brinkhof, Edwin Dijkman, Dirk Hooglandt, Tamara Santing, Hinke Wever, Dick Barten, Heske Berkenkamp, Harm van der Geest, Dick Kuijs, Willem Lohy, Leon van Mil, Tijn Sardée, Carin Tielen, Will Vermeer, Jan L. de Boer, Fran Schreuder, Arenda Woudenberg, Marleen Flobbe, Peter Kuijsters, Arno Francke, Wilfred Reneman, and Mark Eeftens.

About the Author

Journalist, writer, and musician **Hugo Pinksterboer**, author of The Tipbook Series, has published hundreds of interviews, articles, and reviews for national and international music magazines, and contributed to music method books, piano tuner handbooks, courses for music sales people, and a wide variety of other publications.

About the Designer

Illustrator, designer, and musician **Gijs Bierenbroodspot** has worked as an art director for a wide variety of magazines and has developed numerous ad campaigns. While searching in vain for information about saxophone mouthpieces, he got the idea for this series of books on music and musical instruments. He is responsible of the layout and illustrations for all of the Tipbooks.

Acknowledgments

Cover photo: René Vervloet
Editors: Robert L. Doerschuk and Rachel Stevens
Proofreaders: Nancy Bishop and Patricia Waddy

Anything missing?

Any omissions? Any areas that could be improved? Please go to www.tipbook.com to contact us, or send an email to info@tipbook.com. Thanks!

Contents

VII

Introduction

Tipbook Music on Paper – Basic Theory *is a highly accessible introduction to reading music from the very first start, as well as a handy reference guide for advanced players. It explains the basic principles of music theory, from scales and keys to transposition and song forms. Additionally, the book teaches you how to read chord symbols, and it tells you about chord functions and harmony. So here is all you need to know to handle any score, to understand the basics of the composition, and to play it the way it was intended.*

The first chapter tells you why reading music can help you become a better musician, and it takes you on a tour along the other chapters. The basic idea behind the book is not only to help you read music, but to provide a better understanding of what you are playing. Understanding the music, rather than simply executing the written notes in the prescribed order, helps you become a better musician — and in turn, it makes reading the actual notes easier as well!

The next step
The knowledge collected in this book, with the help of the many musicians listed on page V, also prepares you for the next step, offering information that helps you to transcribe and transpose music, or even to write or arrange your own music, or to improve your solo playing.

Any style

Tipbook Music on Paper has not been written with a specific style of music in mind. On the contrary, this Tipbook and all other Tipbooks are intended for instrumentalists and vocalists at any level and in any style of music, from classical music to rock and jazz. We're proud to say that they're used and loved by musicians from all of those backgrounds, ranging from heavy metal guitarists to members of senior citizen choirs, jazz drummers, and conservatory students, and from absolute beginners to advanced musicians.

Examples

To make the music come to life, this Tipbook is full of easy-to-play examples and practical tips — not just about theory, but about music. Should you not have a keyboard instrument at hand, most of the musical examples in the examples can be listened to at www.tipbook.com. (See pages XII–XIV for more information.)

Reference

You can read *Tipbook Music on Paper* chapter by chapter, but we also wanted it to be a quick reference. So there's a glossary that briefly explains most of the musical terms that you come across on the following pages, there is a complete index that helps you to trace the information you're looking for, and an *Essential Reference* with memory joggers and all kinds of helpful items. As an extra, a list of musical symbols has been printed on the inside covers of the book, the numbers referring to the pages where these symbols are explained. Quick, handy, and to the point, so you can spend more time playing. Enjoy!

— Hugo Pinksterboer and Bart Noorman

See and Hear What You Read with Tipcodes

www.tipbook.com

In addition to the many illustrations on the following pages, Tipbooks offer you a new way to see — and even hear — what you are reading about. The Tipcodes that you will come across regularly in this book give you access to extra pictures, short videos, sound files, and other additional information at www. tipbook.com.

Here's how it works: On page 35 of this book, there is a paragraph on quintuplets and septuplets. Below this paragraph is **Tipcode MOP-016**. Type in that code on the Tipcode page at www.tipbook. com and you will hear what a quintuplet and a septuplet sound like. Similar audio examples are available on a wide variety of subjects; other Tipcodes will link to a short video.

Tipcode MOP-016

Tipcodes listed

For your convenience, the Tipcodes presented in this book are listed on page pages 204–205. The Tipcodes in this book mainly include demonstrations of a wide range of musical instruments, ranging from the clarinet voices to violin and viola, nylon-string and steel-string guitars, flutes, and drums.

Plug-ins

If the software you need to view the videos is not yet installed on your computer, you'll automatically be told which software you need, and where you can download it. This type of software is free. Questions? Check out 'About this site' at www.tipbook.com.

Still more at www.tipbook.com

You can find even more information at www.tipbook.com. For instance, you can look up words in the glossaries of all the Tipbooks published to date. There are chord diagrams for guitarists and pianists; fingering charts for saxophonists, clarinetists, and flutists; and rudiments for drummers. Also included are links to most of the websites mentioned in the *Want to Know More?* section of each Tipbook.

First, make your selection: Tipcode, chords and fingering charts, or the glossary.

The Tipcode window displays movies, photo series, fingering charts, chords, and explanations of the words used in this book.

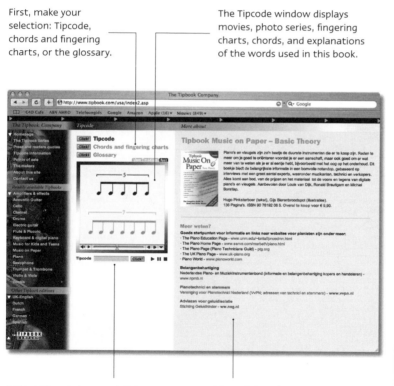

Enter a Tipcode here and click on the button. Want to see it again? Click again.

These links take you directly to other interesting sites.

1

Music on Paper

Learning to read music is not much harder than it was to learn reading text. You started off with one letter at a time, then moved up to reading words, and gradually you learned how to handle entire phrases at a glance. And just like learning to read text, learning to read music takes a little time at first, but it definitely pays off in the end. Here is how to get the most out of this book.

Outside of the classical world, there are many well-known musicians who have never read a note of music in their lives. Thousands of bands in all kinds of popular styles of music never use sheet music, and there are thousands of songs thought up by musicians who never put anything on paper. So why should you want to learn to read music?

- You'll have access to **loads of sheet music**, including songs and pieces by your favorite band or composer, as well as exercises, etudes, and so on.

- If sheet music is provided, you can basically **play along** with any group at your musical level without prior rehearsals.

- You can also **write music**: exercises and tunes, a part for the bass player or the brass section, an idea for a solo, and so on. Writing something down is easier than remembering it, especially in the long run.

- It makes communicating with other musicians a lot easier. You'll **never be dumbstruck** by talk of a B♭ major scale, a fifth, a triplet, or the Mixolydian mode.

- It makes it easier to **understand how music is structured** — from single chords to whole pieces — and how and why it works the way it does.

By heart
Being able to read music doesn't mean you always have to play from sheet music. Classical musicians usually do, but music stands

TIP

Reading tabs
A growing number of guitarists and bassists don't learn how to read traditional notation. Instead, they use tabs, and guitarists use chord diagrams as well (see Chapter 19). If you play one of these instruments and you're serious about making music, it's well worth it to pick up on traditional notation too. Tabs and chord diagrams show you which fingers to use on which strings — but not a whole lot more than that.

2

are rare on rock, blues, and folk stages. Sheet music allows you to play things that others have written, but once you know a piece by heart, it may very well sound better if you play it without the music: You'll be able to focus on how the notes are supposed to sound, rather than on which notes you're supposed to play.

The numbers in the black circles indicate the relevant chapter for each subject.

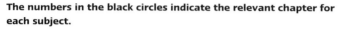

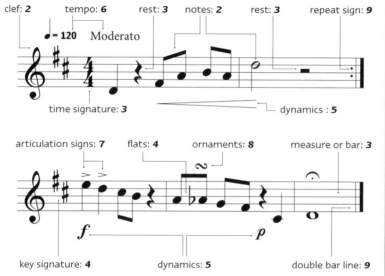

The clef and the staff: **Chapter 2**

The higher the position of a note on the staff, the higher it sounds: **Chapter 2**

The looks of notes and rests tell you how long they last: **Chapter 3**

The number of beats per bar, and which note lasts one beat: **Chapter 3**

Notes can be raised or lowered a half tone by using sharps and flats: **Chapter 4**

Dynamic markings tell you to play loud, or soft, or at any volume level in between: **Chapter 5**

Tempo indications show how fast a piece should be played: **Chapter 6**

Accents and other articulation markings show how a note should be 'pronounced': **Chapter 7**

Ornaments are used to embellish notes: **Chapter 8**

Repeat signs tell you to repeat one or more bars: **Chapter 9**

A GUIDE

If you don't read music yet, check out the first eight chapters —
but note that they contain advanced subjects as well, ranging from
C clefs to quintuplets, diatonic half steps, scoops, and doits. Note
that such topics are typically introduced at the end of a chapter or
section, so you can easily skip them at first!

Two to nine
Chapters 2 to 4 look at how high or low the notes sound (pitch),
how long they last, and when to play them. Chapters 5 to 8 tell you
how you should play them: loud, soft, fast or slow, accented, or
embellished. Chapter 9 covers repeat signs and navigation markers. The guide on the previous page summarizes where each bit of
information can be found.

Ten to fourteen
Chapters 10 to 14 explain the system behind the notes. You don't
necessarily need all this information to read music note by note,
but it definitely helps you to really understand what you're playing.

Fifteen and onwards
Chapters 15 to 21 are extras, covering chords, transposition,
unusual meters, swing, the clave, alternative ways to put music on
paper, musical notation for drummers, tips on writing out music,
and a brief history of music notation.

*A basic, small
keyboard is
all you need
to play the
examples
in this book.*

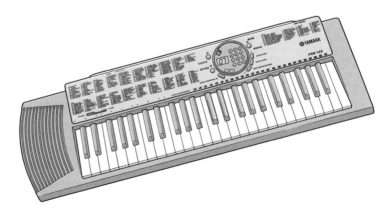

Home keyboard

Having a keyboard instrument at hand makes this book even more valuable. Most musical examples on the following pages can be easily played by non-pianists, as long as you carefully read the accompanying text. In most cases, you can even play them using one finger only! To play the examples, a very basic home keyboard will do, and you can get one for as little as fifty to a hundred dollars — or see if you can borrow one first.

Tipcodes

If you don't have a keyboard instrument at hand, you can still listen to most of the musical examples in this book by using the unique Tipcodes. Simply type in the code on the Tipcode page at www.tipbook.com and hear what you are reading about! See pages XII–XIV for additional information.

Compositions and numbers

A piece of classical music is usually called a *composition*. Pop songs, jazz standards, and other compositions are usually referred to as *songs* or *tunes*. In this book, the neutral term 'piece' is used in most cases, for compositions in any style of music. A *chart*, *part*, or *score* contains the written music for a specific instrument. The word score is also often used to indicate the conductor's sheet music, which shows all the parts in a piece.

'Twinkle, Twinkle, Little Star'

This book begins with 'Twinkle, Twinkle, Little Star' and it uses a few other well-known children's songs as well. Why? Simply because almost everyone knows them, and it's a lot easier to grasp what you read if you already know what it's supposed to sound like.

Western and non-Western music

Tipbook Music on Paper – Basic Theory deals with what's generally known as Western music: music that typically originates from Europe and North America. Non-Western music can be heard increasingly often in Western countries, either in its pure, authentic form or mixed with Western elements, the latter generally known as fusion or world music. In many cases, different rules apply to the original musical styles from other cultures, ranging

5

from different notation to completely different ways to compose or structure the music.

2

High and Low

Music is made up of shorter and longer notes, and higher and lower sounding notes. Bass guitars and tubas play the lower notes, violins and flutes play higher notes, and pianos and organs can play both low and high notes. A piece of music clearly shows the higher and the lower notes: The higher notes are simply printed higher on the five-lined staff, while the lower notes sit lower on the staff.

On a keyboard instrument, every note has its own key. Having such an instrument at hand is of great help for the following introduction and the next chapters (see pages 4–5).

Twinkle, Twinkle
If you sing 'Twinkle, Twinkle, Little Star,' the second 'Twinkle' sounds higher than the first. If you play it on a keyboard instrument, you'll see that you find the higher sounding notes by moving to the right along the keyboard. If you move to the left, you'll play lower sounding notes.

'Twinkle, Twinkle, Little Star': *Each syllable is a note.*

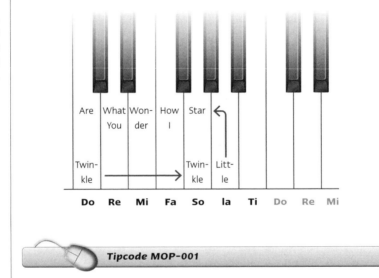

Tipcode MOP-001

On the keyboard
The diagram above shows you how to play 'Twinkle, Twinkle' on a keyboard instrument. Simply press one key per syllable, and you will soon recognize the melody.

Higher is faster
If you sing along, your vocal folds will vibrate faster when you sing the higher notes ('Litt-le'), and slower when singing the lower notes ('Twinkle'). Likewise, if you play the piano or the guitar, its strings will vibrate faster as you play higher sounding notes.

8

> ## Rubber band
>
> *If you don't have a piano or a guitar at hand, take a rubber*
> *band. Stretch it between two fingers, and make it vibrate*
> *as if it were a string. Listen to the pitch. Now stretch it a bit*
> *further, and play it again. You will see that it vibrates faster,*
> *and you will hear a higher pitch.*

TIP

The octave
If you sing Do Re Mi Fa Sol La Ti Do, the final Do ('Doh') will
make your vocal folds sound twice as fast as the first, lower Do. In
musical terms: The high Do sounds an *octave* higher than the first.

Tipcode MOP-002

The same, but higher
The high Do is the same note as the low Do, as these names
suggest, but it has a higher pitch. When you play these two notes
simultaneously on a piano, you'll hardly hear that you're playing
two notes. They seem to blend in with each other.

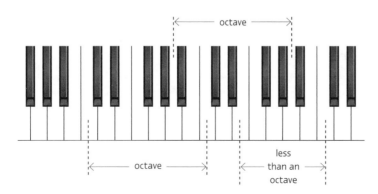

Octaves on a keyboard.

Like one
Take another look at the keyboard on page 8. First play the lowest
Do (at 'Twinkle'), then play the high Do. You will hear an octave.
Now play them together, and they'll sound like one.

9

Eight white keys

If you go from Do to the next Do, you'll count eight white keys. These keys are known as the *white notes*. An octave encompasses eight white notes.

Tipcode MOP-003

Letter names

You can use the syllables Do, Re, Mi (etc.) to indicate the white notes or *natural notes*, but they're typically known by their letter names: C, D, E, F, G, A, and B.

The natural notes or white notes on a keyboard.

C to C

As the keyboard above shows you, the B is followed by a higher C, and then the entire range is repeated. From one C to the next is an octave; from one D to the next D is an octave too, and so on.

Alphabet

You may have noticed that the order of the white notes is identical to the order of the letters of the alphabet, the only difference being that this range now starts at C instead of A.

Black keys

A keyboard has black keys too. If you go from key to key, white and black, from left to right, every next note will sound a *half step* or a *half tone* higher. On a piano keyboard, a half step is the smallest distance between two notes. There are *twelve* half steps in an octave.

Tipcode MOP-004

Whole steps

If you go from one white key to the next, the diagram below shows that you play both half steps and *whole steps*.

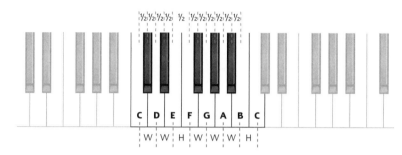

From key to key: half steps (H). From white key to white key: whole (W) and half (H) steps.

No black key

If you look at the keyboard, you will see that there are no black keys between the natural notes E and F, and between B and C. In other words: From E to F is a half step, and from B to C is a half step. There is a whole step between all other neighboring white notes, from C to D, and so on.

Finding your way

The black keys on a keyboard are laid out in alternate groups of two and three. This layout makes it very easy to find you way on the instrument. All you need to remember is that:

• The white key to the left of **two** black keys is a **C**.

• The white key to the left of **three** black keys is an **F**.

Knowing the alphabet now allows you to find the other white notes as well.

Middle C and the other Cs

The C in the middle of a piano keyboard is known as Middle C. The same key is also referred to as C4: It's the fourth C on the instrument, counting from the left (see page 214).

TIP

11

Guitar

You can play all white notes — and octaves, and whole and half steps, on almost any other instrument as well. The guitar, for example.

- If you slide your finger upward from fret to fret (from the top of the neck toward the body), you'll be moving up in **half steps**.

- If you skip one fret each time, you will be playing **whole steps**.

- If you move up twelve frets (twelve half steps), you will play an **octave**.

Whole steps, half steps, and an octave on guitar.

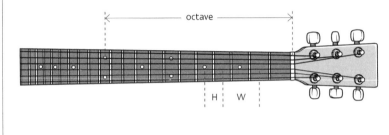

ON PAPER

Written music or sheet music shows you which notes to play, and how long each note should last.

The staff

Music is typically written on a *staff* or *stave*: a set of five horizontal lines. You count these lines from the bottom up, so the top line is the fifth line.

Higher, lower

The higher a note is written on the staff, the higher it sounds. Lower-sounding notes sit lower on the staff. Easy!

Up, down, and to the right.

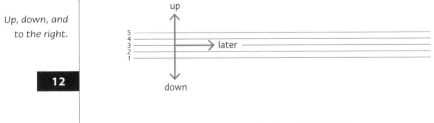

Left to right
You read and play the notes from left to right, just like text.

On paper
The following example shows you what 'Twinkle, Twinkle' looks like in notes. When the melody goes up, the notes on the staff go up too. And as the tune goes down (from 'little'), the corresponding notes sit lower on the staff.

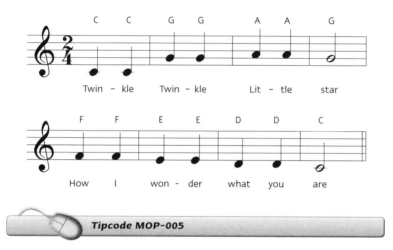

Music on paper: Higher sounding notes sit higher on the staff.

How long
You can also see that the longer sounding notes at the end of each phrase ('star' and 'are') look different from the other notes: These two longer notes have an open *head*, while the others have a solid notehead. This is dealt with in Chapter 3.

Lines and spaces
A staff can house eleven notes. They can be written

- **on** the lines (the line runs through the note);
- **between** the lines;
- or below or **below or above** the lines.

The notes on the lines.

13

The notes between, below and above the lines.

Eleven notes on the staff.

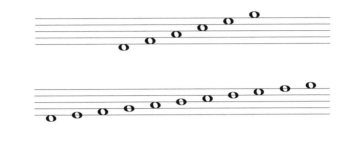

CLEFS

Clarinets, violins, saxophones, and most other *melody instruments* can play at least some thirty different notes. A piano has no less than eighty-eight keys, making for just as many different notes. So clearly, one five-lined staff is not sufficient to house all these different notes. That's why there are staffs with different *clefs*.

G clef and F clef

The clef is the symbol at the beginning of a staff. The two most common clefs are the curly G clef and the F clef, which looks somewhat like a big comma.

Treble clef

The staff with the *G clef* is used for higher sounding notes: Music for higher sounding instruments, such as trumpets and flutes, is written on a staff with a G clef. Therefore it's also known as the *treble clef*.

Treble clef or G clef.

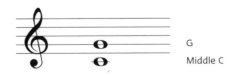

G

Middle C

Curl

The curl of the G clef or treble clef indicates the note G above Middle C. Middle C is on a separate line below this staff.

Bass clef

The staff with the *F clef* is used for lower sounding instruments, such as the double bass, the bass guitar, or the tuba. Therefore it's also known as the *bass clef*.

Middle C

F

Bass clef or F clef.

Two dots

The two dots of the F clef indicate the note F below Middle C. Middle C is above this staff.

Notes and keys

Below, you see a series of piano keys and the corresponding notes on both staffs. Middle C is on a small extra line below the treble staff, and on a similar line above the bass staff.

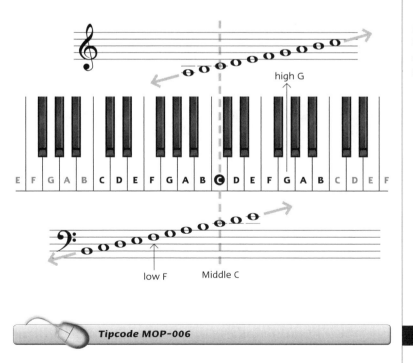

high G

E F G A B C D E F G A B C D E F G A B C D E F

low F   Middle C

Natural notes in the bass (F) and treble (G) clefs.

Tipcode MOP-006

TIPBOOK MUSIC ON PAPER

Different

So the notes sit on different places on each staff. For example, the middle line of the treble staff indicates a B. The middle line of the bass clef indicates a D.

TIP

Memory joggers

Here are two popular memory joggers to help you remember the names of the notes on the lines for both clefs.

- *G clef, first to fifth line: **E**very **G**ood **B**ird **D**oes **F**ly*

- *F clef, first to fifth line: **G**ood **B**irds **D**o **F**ly, **A**lways.*

  And for the spaces:

- *G clef, first to fourth space: **F A C E***

- *F clef, first to fourth space: **A**ll **C**ows **E**at **G**rass*

One or both staffs

Most musicians only need to learn to read the notes in one of these staffs. If you play the piano or another keyboard instrument you'll have to read both staffs simultaneously: the one with a bass clef for the lower sounding notes you play with your left hand, and the treble clef for the higher sounding notes you usually play with your right hand. Harpists also have to read both staffs.

Pianists read two staffs simultaneously: Here's a bit of salsa for advanced players.

Tipcode MOP-007

C clef
There is yet another clef, the *C clef*. This clef indicates Middle C. Contrary to the other clefs, it is a *movable clef*. It can assign the note C to any of the five lines of the staff.

Tenor staff
Music for cellists, for example, may have the C clef indicating Middle C on the fourth line. This is known as the *tenor staff*. (Cellists use the treble and bass clefs too.)

soprano clef   mezzo-soprano clef   alto clef   tenor clef   baritone clef

The C-clef or moveable clef: Middle C can be assigned to any line.

Alto, soprano, and more
If you play the viola or if you're an alto singer, your music may be printed on an *alto staff*, with the C clef indicating Middle C on the third line. Likewise, there is a *soprano staff*, a *mezzo-soprano staff*, and a *baritone staff*.

Treble clef
Most examples in this book use the treble clef.

EXTENDING THE STAFFS

Using different clefs isn't enough to print the highest and the lowest notes. Therefore, the staffs can be extended in two ways: using ledger lines, or with an instruction that tells you to play one or two octaves above or below the written notes.

Ledger lines
Each staff can be extended with the so-called ledger lines. Middle

17

C is always on a *ledger line*, either right below the treble staff or above the bass staff.

Notes on ledger lines.

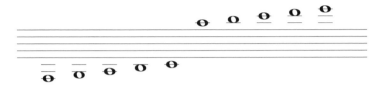

Octave higher or lower

Notes with three or more ledger lines are quite hard to read. The solution is simple: Instead of printing notes way above or below the staff, you're told to play an octave — or even two octaves — higher or lower than the written pitches.

• The abbreviation **8va** (ottava alta) or the number 8 printed above a note instructs you to play this note and all following notes an octave higher than written.

• The abbreviation **8va bassa**, or 8vb or the number 8 below a note tells you to play an octave lower.

• Likewise, **15ma and 15mb** (quindicesima alta, quindicesima bassa) make you play two octaves higher and lower respectively.

Two ways of writing the same melody. The one below is much easier to read.

Loco

A dotted or dashed line usually tells you how long to continue this transposition, as shown above. If there's no line, you go on until you see the Italian word *loco* ('in place').

Guitars and piccolos

The guitar and some other instruments sound an octave lower than the written notes indicate. An 8 may be printed below the clef to make sure the music is played correctly. This is known as an octave clef. *For instruments that sound an octave higher than the written pitches, such as the piccolo, a small 8 can be printed above the clef.*

Transposing instruments

Most wind instruments sound different notes than the written pitches. An example: If you play the tenor saxophone and there is a C in your chart, you will finger a C — but the pitch you will hear is a whole step lower. This is because the tenor saxophone, like most other wind instruments, is a *transposing instrument*. There's more about this in Chapter 15. Non-transposing instruments are said to play in *concert pitch*: They sound the written pitch.

Chords

On keyboard instruments, guitars, and many other stringed instruments, you can play *chords*: three or more notes played simultaneously. On paper, the notes of a chord are aligned vertically. If two notes occupy adjacent places on the staff, they can't be aligned vertically, so they're printed very close to one another instead. There's more about chords in Chapter 18.

A chord is a number of notes played simultaneously.

Tipcode MOP-008

3

Long and Short

The position of a note on the staff shows you which note to play. The look of the note itself tells you how long it's supposed to last.

Whether you are listening to drum 'n' bass, a symphony orchestra, jazz, or country, you can always tap your foot in time to what you hear. Once every few taps you may hear or feel some sort of accent. Just sing the two following songs:

1 - 2　**1** - 2　**1** - 2　**1** - 2
Yan - kee **Doo** - dle **went**　to　**town**　–

1 - 2 - 3　**1** - 2 - 3　**1** - 2 - 3
My **Bon** - nie　lies　**o** - ver　the　**o** - cean　–

Oompa

The 'accents' in 'Yankee Doodle' subdivide the song into groups of *two* taps or beats. 'My Bonnie' is divided into groups of *three* beats. These subdivisions make for the rhythmic feel of the music. Dance to it and you'll feel it: *oompa oompa* makes you move differently than *oompapa oompapa* does.

Bars

Most music is divided into such groups of two, three, or four beats. Each group of beats is called a *bar* or a *measure*.

THE NOTES

If you clap along as you sing the first four words of 'Baa Baa Black Sheep' you will probably clap on each word. 'Baa Baa Black Sheep' is four beats.

Tipcode MOP-009

Quarter note

If you look at the musical example below, you will see that each of the first four beats of the song is represented by a black round notehead with a stem, known as a quarter note. In the majority of songs and classical pieces, the *quarter note* represents one beat.

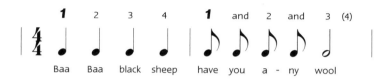

Four in a bar

Many of those songs and compositions have four beats to every bar, each beat equaling a quarter (¼) note. This is shown at the beginning of the staff as ¼, pronounced as *four-four time*. 'Baa Baa Black Sheep' is in ¼, as you can see.

Bar line

The example above shows two bars, separated by a vertical line. This is a *bar line*.

Shorter and longer notes

The first bar contains four quarter notes, equaling four beats. The second bar contains four shorter notes and one longer note. The four shorter notes are *eighth notes* (equaling half beats); the longer note is a *half note* (equals two beats). Together, they equal four quarter notes or beats: ½ + ½ + ½ + ½ + 2 = 4.

Note values

There are notes with even higher and lower *note values* as well, from the whole note to thirty-second notes and even shorter notes.

The whole note: four beats in ¼

The longest note you can play in a four beat bar is the *whole note*. The *whole* note fills up the *whole* bar. If you play a whole note on

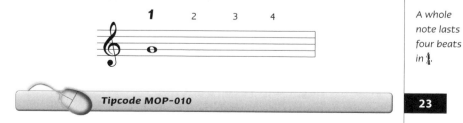

A whole note lasts four beats in ¼.

Tipcode MOP-010

a keyboard, you hold the key down for all four beats. On a wind instrument, you keep blowing for four beats. Tapping your foot, one tap per beat, will help you counting out the note.

The half note: two beats in ⁴⁄₄

The *half note* lasts half as long as a whole note: two beats. Two half notes fill up a four-beat bar.

The half note: two beats in ⁴⁄₄.

The quarter note: one beat in ⁴⁄₄

In ⁴⁄₄, the *quarter note* lasts one beat. If you tap along with your foot, play one note to each tap.

The quarter note: one beat in ⁴⁄₄.

The eighth note: half a beat in ⁴⁄₄

There are two *eighth notes* in one quarter note. In 'Baa Baa Black Sheep' the words 'have you any' are eighth notes: There are two notes for each beat. You can count these eighth notes out loud in various ways. Here are some examples:

An eighth note lasts half a beat in ⁴⁄₄.

Sixteenth note: a quarter beat in ⁴⁄₄

There are four *sixteenth notes* to one beat in ⁴⁄₄. Sixteenth notes sound twice as fast as eighth notes. Four sixteenths last as long as one quater note. Here are some ways to count them:

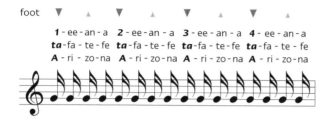

A sixteenth note lasts a quarter of a beat in ¼.

Even shorter notes
You rarely see them, but there are thirty-second notes and sixty-fourth notes (etc.) as well.

Sixty-fourth notes: sixteen notes equaling one quarter note.

Heads, stems, and flags
Notes are made up of one, two, or three parts: an open or a closed head, a stem, and a flag:

The note	Its name	Its parts	Lasts (in ¼)
o	whole note (semibreve)	open head	four beats
𝅗𝅥	half note (minim)	open head and stem	two beats
𝅘𝅥	quarter note (crotchet)	closed head and stem	one beat
𝅘𝅥𝅮	eighth note (quaver)	closed head, stem, and flag	half a beat
𝅘𝅥𝅯	sixteenth note (semiquaver)	closed head, stem, and two flags	quarter beat

British note names
Most British and Australian musicians use different note names. The table above shows these British names in parentheses. The

British names for thirty-second and sixty-fourth notes are *demisemiquaver* and *hemidemisemiquaver* respectively.

TIP

Cross-shaped noteheads

Next to notes with regular closed or open noteheads, you may come across other notehead shapes as well. In drum charts, cross-shaped noteheads indicate cymbals (see page 174). In other charts, they can either tell you to play ghost notes (see page 68), or use another effect, such as hitting the soundbox of your guitar. In a vocal chart, lyrics with cross-style noteheads are spoken, rather than sung, the way rap artists typically do. The classical term for this technique is Sprechgesang.

TIME SIGNATURES

'Baa Baa Black Sheep' is in ⁴⁄₄ or four-four time, as you saw on pages 22–23. This is the *time signature* of the song. It tells you how many beats there are in each bar, and which note equals one beat.

Four-four bar
In a piece in ⁴⁄₄, each bar lasts as long as four quarter notes. So it may contain four quarter notes, but also one whole note, or two quarter notes and a half note, and so on, as long as it all adds up to ⁴⁄₄.

Upper number
The upper number of the time signature tells you the number of beats per bar. In a piece in ⁴⁄₄ there are four beats in each bar.

Lower number and counting unit
The lower number indicates which note lasts one beat. In ⁴⁄₄, that's a quarter note: ¼ + ¼ + ¼ + ¼ = ⁴⁄₄. This implies that you count the piece in quarter notes: The quarter note is the *counting unit*.

Three-four

Another popular time signature is $\frac{3}{4}$ (three-four time or *waltz time*). There are three beats to every bar, and each beat equals a quarter note. The quarter note is the counting unit. 'My Bonnie Lies Over the Ocean' is a well-known example.

My   Bon - nie   lies   o - ver   the

'My Bonnie': three beats per bar.

Two or five

There are more time signatures than just $\frac{4}{4}$ and $\frac{3}{4}$. For example, time signatures with two beats per bar, such as $\frac{2}{4}$; (e.g., 'Twinkle, Twinkle') or five beats per bar, such as $\frac{5}{4}$.

Another counting unit

Likewise, there are time signatures with another counting unit, usually the eighth note. $\frac{3}{8}$ has three beats to every bar, and the eighth note is the counting unit.

c and ¢

Instead of $\frac{4}{4}$, the symbol c is used quite often. It's the C of 'common' time. The symbol ¢ indicates a $\frac{2}{2}$ time signature, which is also known as *cut common time* or *alla breve*. In $\frac{2}{2}$, the half note is the counting unit; a half note equals one beat. There's more about time signatures in Chapter 16.

BEAMS

Groupings of eighth notes, sixteenth notes, and shorter notes can be made easier to read if their individual flags are replaced by *beams*.

Beam = flag

A beam has the same value as a flag. An eighth note has one flag,

Individual notes make this melody hard to read.

The same melody: Beams group the notes and make them easier to read.

so eighth notes are joined by a single beam. Sixteenth notes have two flags, so they're joined with a double beam.

One beat

A group of notes joined by a single or a multiple beam typically represents the value of one beat, as shown above: In 4/4, beams join groups of two eighth notes, or four sixteenth notes. The first note of each group always falls on the beat, again making the music easier to read than it would be with individual notes.

One whole note, two half notes, four quarter notes, eight eighth notes, sixteen sixteenth notes: They all last four beats in 4/4, filling up one bar.

Single and double beams

Single and double beams can be combined in one group. In the examples below, each group has two sixteenths and one eighth note. This adds up to the value of one quarter note: $2/16 + 1/8 = 1/4$.

1-**ee**-an-a   1-**ee**-an-a

Combining single and double beams.

Flags for vocalists

If a vocalist is supposed to sing a different note for each syllable, flags are used rather than beams. If a syllable is spread over a number of notes of different pitches (a *melisma*), beams are used instead of flags.

RESTS

Each of the preceding examples assigns one or more notes to every beat. However, there's more to music than notes. The rests are just as important: silence, next to sound. A rest means you actually stop playing for a moment. Rests have the same time values as notes: There are whole rests, half rests, quarter rests, and shorter rests.

Rectangles and tags

In $\frac{4}{4}$, a *whole rest* lasts four beats, just like a whole note. It looks like a small solid rectangle, hanging from the fourth line on the staff.

- The **half rest** is a similar rectangle sitting on the third line.

- The **quarter rest** or quarter-note rest looks like a Z over a capital C.

- The **shorter rests**, starting with the eighth rest, consist of a slash and one or more tags or hooks: the more hooks, the shorter the rest. One hook between the third and fourth line, indicates an eighth rest.

29

The rest	Its name	Lasts as long as		Beats in $\frac{4}{4}$
▬	whole rest	○	whole note	four beats
▬	half rest (minim rest)	♩	half note	two beats
𝄽	quarter rest (crotchet rest)	♩	quarter note	one beat
𝄾	eighth rest (quaver rest)	♪	eighth note	half a beat
𝄿	sixteenth rest (semiquaver rest)	♬	sixteenth note	quarter beat

TIP

Whole rest

The whole rest is different from the whole note: a whole rest always tells you to be silent for that whole bar, no matter what the time signature is. It equals four beats in $\frac{4}{4}$, but also six beats in $\frac{6}{8}$ or nine in $\frac{9}{8}$.

Two or four

You rarely see them, but there are symbols to indicate a rest that lasts for two or four bars. The figure 2 may be printed above the two-bar *breve rest*, while a 4 indicates the number of bars for a *long rest*. The breve rest is also used to indicate a one bar rest in $\frac{4}{2}$.

A breve rest and a long rest.

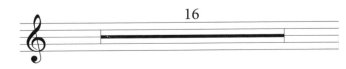

Multiple bars

If you're supposed to keep quiet for a larger number of bars, you'll see a *multiple measure rest* or *multi-measure rest* with the exact number of bars specified above it.

A sixteen-bar rest.

16

General pause

The letters GP stand for *general pause* or *grand pause*, indicating a generally unexpected moment of silence for all musicians. The duration is determined by the conductor.

DOTS AND TIES

So far you've seen symbols that represent the time values of notes and rests: four beats, two beats, one beat, and so on. But there are also notes of other lengths: a beat-and-a-half, for example, or three beats. There are two ways to write such notes: with *dots* and with *ties*.

The dot

Printing a dot after a note makes it last 1.5 times as long. In ¾ a half note with a dot lasts 1.5 x two beats = three beats. A dotted quarter note lasts a beat-and-a-half, and so on. These dots are known as *augmentation dots*.

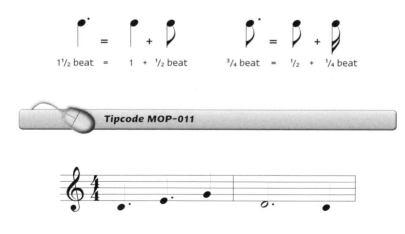

1½ beat = 1 + ½ beat   ³/₄ beat = ½ + ¼ beat

Adding a dot makes a note sound 1.5 times as long.

Tipcode MOP-011

Dotted notes in a melody.

Two dots

Notes can have two dots too, the second dot adding half of the duration of the first dot: in ¾ a double-dotted half note lasts 2 + 1 + ½ = three-and-a-half beats.

31

A double-dotted half note.

3¹/₂ beats = 2 + 1 + ¹/₂ beat

Rests
Rests can be dotted and double-dotted as well.

Dotted rests.

Ties
A *tie* extends a note by joining it to another note of the same pitch. These two notes are then played as one longer note.

Ties join notes.

1¹/₂ beats   2¹/₂ beats 1 beat   4¹/₂ beats

Tipcode MOP-012

Dots or ties?
Dotted notes may be easier to read then tied notes, but ties allow for a few things that dots don't. Two examples:

• Ties can make a note last into **the following bar**. Dots can't.

• Ties allow for notes that last, say, **two-and-a-half beats**, as shown above.

In other words: Dots offer less options than ties.

TUPLETS

As you have seen, each note can be divided into two, four, eight, or more shorter notes. But you can also divide notes into three or

32

five, for example. Collectively, these subdivided notes are known as *tuplets*.

Triplets

If you divide a quarter note into two, you get two eighth notes. When you divide it into three, you get an *eighth-note triplet*. Triplets are marked with the figure 3 above or below the three notes, sometimes with an additional square bracket or a slur that groups the notes. If you have to play a long sequence of triplets, only the first triplet(s) may have these markers.

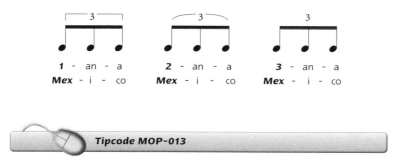

Two ways to count eighth-note triplets, and three ways to write them.

Tipcode MOP-013

Sixteenth-note triplets

Sixteenth-note triplets are formed by dividing eighth notes into three. Below are two examples of an eight note plus a sixteenth note triplet, each equaling a quarter note.

An eighth note followed by a sixteenth-note triplet, and vice versa.

Quarter-note triplets

A *quarter-note triplet* is what you get if a half note is divided into three quarter notes. It takes time to learn to play quarter-note triplets, since you have to play three notes while counting two beats (see page 148).

Tipcode MOP-014

33

TIP

Three in the time of two

When you play triplets, you play three notes in the same amount of time it would normally take to play two of such notes. In other words: An eighth note triplet is three notes in the time of two eighth notes; a quarter note triplet is three notes in the time of two quarter notes, etc.

Not always all three

You don't always play all three notes of a triplet, of course. Below are some eighth-note triplets with one note missing:

Two notes as a single note

A composer can also require you to play two adjacent notes of a triplet as a single, longer note. This can be indicated by changing the note value or by using a tie.

Different notations, same sound.

Sextuplets

Notes can also be divided into six: the *sextuplet.*

A quarter note divided into six: a sixteenth-note sextuplet.

Tipcode MOP-015

DadadaDadada

34

Two sixteenth-note triplets seem very similar to a sextuplet, but there is a difference. Two sixteenth-note triplets are usually felt as two groups of three (DadadaDadada). A sextuplet usually feels more like three groups of two (DadaDadaDada) or one group of six (Dadadadadada).

Da – da – da   Da – da – da   Da – da – Da – da – Da – da

The difference: two sixteenth-note triplets and a sextuplet.

Five or seven

It may take a little while to get used to the slightly different feel of triplets and sextuplets, but in fact they're very common. Other subdivisions, such as the *quintuplet* (a note divided into five) and the *septuplet* (seven) are much less common in Western music.

Eighth-note quintuplet and septuplet.

Tipcode MOP-016

Duplet and quadruplet

A *duplet* can be seen as the 'opposite' of a triplet: a duplet is two notes in the time of three. The example shows a duplet in ⅜, so you play two notes in the time of three eighth notes. In a *quadruplet*, you play four notes in the time of three.

A duplet in ⅜.

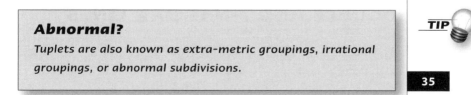

Abnormal?

Tuplets are also known as extra-metric groupings, irrational groupings, or abnormal subdivisions.

TIP

35

PICKUP

The notes and rests in a measure or a bar always equal the number of counting units specified in the time signature: Each bar in a $\frac{4}{4}$ piece contains a combination of notes and rests that add up to the same value as four quarter notes.

Pickup

There is one exception to this rule: The first bar of a piece or a musical phrase may be shorter. Many compositions begin with an 'incomplete' first bar. This is called a *pickup measure*, *pickup*, *upbeat*, or (in the classical world) an *anacrusis*. 'Happy Birthday' and 'My Bonnie' are two well-known examples of songs that start with a pickup measure.

My   Bon - nie   lies   o - ver   the

'My Bonnie Lies Over the Ocean' begins with a pickup. 'My' is the pickup, on the third beat of the incomplete first bar; 'Bonnie' starts on one in the second bar.

The final bar

If there's an incomplete first bar, there's often an incomplete final bar too, adding up to one full bar: If a piece in $\frac{4}{4}$ starts with a one-beat pickup, the final bar may have three beats.

Pickup in a complete bar

Pickups may also appear in the context of a complete bar: If there's a quarter-note pickup, for example, it is preceded by a half rest and a quarter rest.

DOUBLE AND FINAL BAR LINES

Bar lines keep bars apart, making music much easier to read. Next to those regular, single bar lines you will find occasional double bar lines too, and each piece ends with a final bar line.

Double bar line

Many compositions consist of a number of sections of four, eight, sixteen or more bars, separated by *double bar lines*. These double lines are also known as *section lines* or — deceivingly — *double bars*.

Final bar line

The *final bar line* (a regular bar line followed by a thicker one) indicates the end of a piece. The same symbol is also used in various repeat signs, which are explained in Chapter 9.

Double bar line and final bar line.

4

Sharps and Flats

The natural notes or white notes discussed in Chapter 2 are just seven of the twelve notes in an octave. This chapter looks at the other five — the black notes — and explains sharps and flats.

The black notes are lowered or raised white notes. You lower a white note by adding a *flat* (♭); a white note can be raised with a *sharp* (♯).

Examples

For example, a raised G is written as G♯, pronounced as *G sharp*. A lowered G is a G♭ (*G flat*).

Twinkle, Twinkle

The reason to lower or raise notes is best explained with a musical example. With the last two chapters in mind you can now read and play 'Twinkle, Twinkle.' Your ears will tell you if you've got it right.

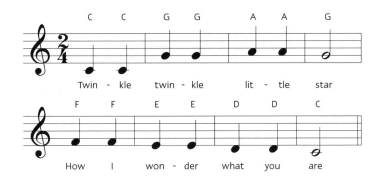

From C to C

This version of 'Twinkle, Twinkle' begins with two Cs. For the next two notes (G), you go five white keys up. From there, you move up one more white key (A), and than you go down the white notes, key by key, ending up again on C.

From F to F

If every piece of music began and ended on C, life would be pretty monotonous. So why not begin 'Twinkle, Twinkle' on another note, say, on F? If you do so and follow the same route as if you'd started in C, you'll hear that something goes wrong. The B, on the words 'how I,' sounds too high. This is perfectly demonstrated in Tipcode MOP–017.

Tipcode MOP-017

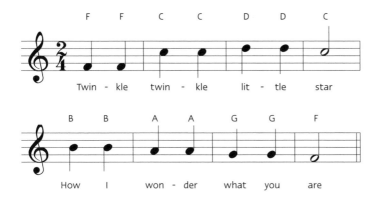

'Twinkle,
Twinkle'
starting on
F. The Bs on
'How I' sound
too high.

Lowering a note

The solution is to lower the B by a half step. On a keyboard you play this lowered B by hitting the black key just to the left of it.

Flats

The lowered B is referred to as B♭ (B flat). To play a flatted note on a keyboard instrument, you simply go one black or white key to the left. That note sounds a half step lower. Here is 'Twinkle, Twinkle,' starting on F. Lowering the B to a B♭ makes it sound right.

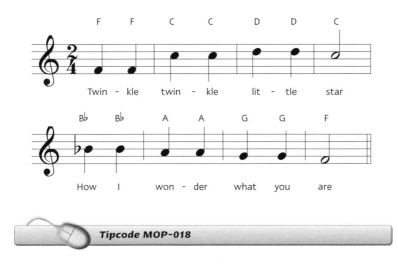

'Twinkle,
Twinkle'
starting on F.
The flat
turns both Bs
into B♭.

Tipcode MOP-018

The other flats

The other natural notes can be lowered exactly the same way.

41

The natural
notes and
the lowered
naturals, or
flats: Cb, Db,
Eb, Fb, Gb,
Ab, Bb.

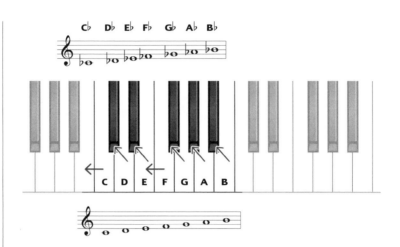

Belly and head

On the staff, the 'belly' of each flat symbol clearly shows which note it refers to: The belly is at the same line or space as the head of that note.

Flats and white keys

Most lowered naturals are played on black keys. The naturals C and F are rarely lowered. But when they are, you play these lowered notes on white keys: As you can see above, Cb uses the same key as B, and Fb is played on the key that's commonly known as E.

SOUNDS FLAT? USE A SHARP!

Conversely, a note that sounds flat (too low) can be raised half a step. If you would begin 'Twinkle, Twinkle' on a D and use white keys only, you'd hear that the F on the word 'wonder' sounds too low.

Too low

The solution is to raise the F a half step. On a keyboard you do so by playing the black note to the right of the F. This is the note F♯ (F sharp).

42

'Twinkle, Twinkle' starting on D. It sounds too low on the word 'wonder'.

'Twinkle, Twinkle' starting on D. The sharp turns the Fs into F♯s.

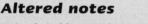
Tipcode MOP-022

Which one?

Each sharp clearly indicates the note you should raise: The middle of each sharp on a staff is at the same line or space as the note it refers to.

E♯ and B♯

Most raised naturals are played on the black keys. The rare notes E♯ and B♯ are played on white keys instead: B♯ is played on the C-

TIP

Altered notes

Raised and lowered notes are known as altered notes: *They are literally altered natural notes.*

43

key, and the E♯ corresponds with the white F-key, as shown on the keyboard below.

lowered (♭)	natural note	raised (♯)
C♭	C	C♯
D♭	D	D♯
E♭	E	E♯
F♭	F	F♯
G♭	G	G♯
A♭	A	A♯
B♭	B	B♯

ACCIDENTALS

Sharps and flats are *chromatic signs*. You may find chromatic signs in one or more bars of a piece, as well as at the very beginning, next to the clef.

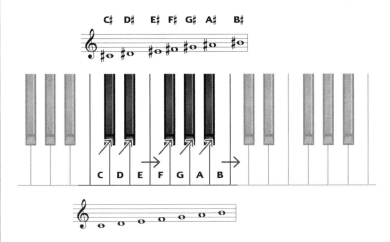

One bar
A sharp or a flat in a bar raises or flattens all following notes of that same pitch in that bar. In 'Twinkle, Twinkle' on D (previous page), a single sharp raises both Fs in the sixth bar.

Accidentals

When used this way, sharps and flats are called *accidentals*. An accidental applies to the notes at the same line or space within the same bar. If there's an accidental before a high F in a bar, it applies to the following high Fs in that bar, but not to a higher or a lower F.

F♯   F♯   F

The third F is not raised because it is a lower F.

One exception

If a note with an accidental is tied over a bar line, the accidental applies to the entire note. It's no longer valid when that note has ended. In the example below, the sharp needs to be repeated in the second bar.

G♯   G♯

An accidental applies throughout a tied note, but not to the rest of the next bar.

KEY SIGNATURE

You'll often see one or more sharps or flats at the very beginning of a piece, next to the clef. These sharps or flats apply to the whole piece and to every octave. If there's one flat next to the clef, every B in the piece should be lowered to B♭, not just the ones at the same line or space as the symbol.

The key of the piece

The sharps or flats at the clef don't just tell you which notes to lower or to raise: They indicate the *key signature* of the piece, or what *key* a piece is in. There's more information on keys and key signatures in Chapters 10 to 14.

45

Every staff

In classical notation, the clef and the key signature are usually repeated at the beginning of every staff. Non-classical composers and arrangers often print it only once, at the beginning of the piece.

Which notes

A key signature may contain none, one, two, three, or more sharps or flats. Each sharp or flat clearly indicates the note it refers to: It is on the same line or space as that note. You can also tell which notes to lower or to raise by looking at the number of flats or sharps: Sharps and flats always appear in a fixed order.

Key signature with two sharps: Every F and C is raised.

Tipcode MOP-019

Always

If there's just one sharp, it raises each F to F♯. If there are two sharps in the key signature, you also raise each C to C♯. Three sharps raise each F, C, and G. This order continues as shown below. The seventh sharp raises each B to B♯.

All sharps in the treble and bass clefs.

All flats in the treble and bass clefs.

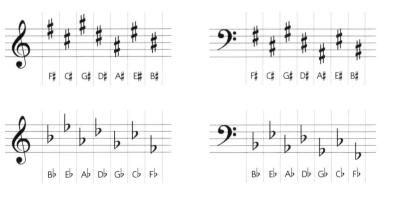

Seven flats

In a piece with one flat, every B turns into a B♭. Two flats flatten every B and E. Again, the order continues, as shown on the opposite page. The seventh flat lowers F to F♭.

Memorize

It's good to memorize these orders, at least up to three or four flats and sharps. (Key signatures with more flats or sharps are rare.) Then, if you see a piece in three flats, for example, you'll know right away that you're supposed to lower all Bs, Es, and As.

System

The fixed orders of flats and sharps are not coincidental. There's a system behind it. Chapter 11 tells you all about it.

Natural signs

Flats and sharps can be suspended within a single bar by the *natural sign* (♮).

Natural sign, turning the key signature's B♭ into a B.

Tipcode MOP-020

Accidentals too

A key signature at the beginning of a piece doesn't mean you won't run into one or more accidentals too, raising or lowering individual notes.

Reminder

Sometimes sharps, flats, and natural signs are printed as reminders, helping to prevent you from hitting the wrong note. These *reminder accidentals* or *cautionary accidentals* often appear in parentheses.

47

ONE NOTE, TWO NAMES

If you take one more look at the two keyboard illustrations on
pages 42 and 44, you'll see that keys can actually have two names.
The middle key in the group of the three black ones is an A♭, if it
happens to be a lowered A. But it can also be a G♯, if it happens to
be a raised G in another song.

Enharmonic notes

Two notes that sound the same, such as A♭ and G♯, are enharmonically equivalent. Enharmonic notes have different names, but you
play them on the same key on a piano, you use the same fingering
on a wind instrument, or you stop a string at the same fret on
a guitar. You'll find other examples of enharmonic notes in the
example below. They also include 'white' notes, of course: B♯ and
C are enharmonic notes for example, and so are F and E.

*Enharmonic
notes: different
names and
looks, but they
sound the same.*

D♯ and E♭   B♯ and C   A♯ and B♭   E and F♭

The key signature

Whether a certain note is a G♯ or an (enharmonic) A♭ depends,
for one thing, on the key signature. The key signature determines
whether notes should be raised or lowered. This was illustrated by
starting 'Twinkle, Twinkle' on different notes, in the beginning of
this chapter. Starting on F required you to flatten all Bs; starting
on D would require you to raise all Fs in the song (and all Cs as
well, should there be any). Chapter 10 tells you the entire story.

Going up, going down

When it comes to accidentals, the direction of the melody often
determines whether a lower note will be raised, or a higher one
flatted. If the melody goes up, the composer is likely to use a sharp.
When the melody descends, it usually makes more sense to use a
flat.

Stepping stone

Here's an example. In the first bar, the direction of the melody is upward, and the G♯ is a stepping stone to the A. In the second bar, the melody descends, and the enharmonic A♭ (which sounds the same as the G♯) leads down to the G.

Tipcode MOP-021

The G♯ and the A♭: same pitch, different name, different effect.

DOUBLE SHARPS AND FLATS

Doubly raised and lowered notes are quite rare, but you may come across them. The *double flat* (♭♭) lowers the natural note by two half steps. The note G preceded by a double-flat is a *G double-flat*, and on a keyboard you play it using the F-key.

Double sharp

The *double-sharp* has its own symbol: 𝄪. It raises a note two half steps. The note G preceded by a double-sharp sign is a G double-sharp. On a keyboard, you play it on the A key.

> ### Chromatic and diatonic
> Sharps and flats are chromatic signs that raise or lower notes by a half step. Going from D to a raised D♯ is therefore known as a chromatic half step. If you go from D to a lowered E (E♭ — the same key as a D♯), however, you're taking a diatonic half step. As a reminder: chromatic half steps have the same note name (C to C♯, G to G♯, for example). Diatonic half steps have different note names (e.g., C to D♭, G to A♭).

49

Why not an A

Why not simply write an A instead of a G𝄪? For the same reason that a G♯ sounds like an A♭, but is, in effect, a different note: It functions either as a raised G or a lowered A. However, as double sharps and flats make reading music quite complicated — unnecessarily complicated, according to many — it's not that unusual to put an A on paper when it's actually supposed to be a G𝄪 or a B♭♭.

5

Loud and Soft

If you play every single note at the same volume, you'll sound more like a machine than a musician. In most styles of music changes in volume — the dynamics — are very important.

The volume level of a sound, or the volume variations in a piece of music, are referred to as dynamics. The composer tells you how loudly or how softly to play by printing dynamic marking in your chart. They're usually abbreviations of a number of Italian terms. Here are some of the standard markings:

Marking	Meaning	In English
ppp	pianississimo; pianissimo possibile	as soft as possible; very, very soft
pp	pianissimo	very soft
p	piano	soft
mp	mezzo piano	moderately soft
mf	mezzo forte	moderately loud
f	forte	loud, strong
ff	fortissimo	very loud; very strong
fff	fortississimo; fortissimo possibile	very, very loud; as loud as possible

Mezzo piano, mezzo forte
The markings above are listed from soft to loud, so *mezzo piano* is softer than *mezzo forte* — but it's a subtle difference.

As loud as possible
Occasionally, you may come across dynamic markings with four or even more letters (such as *ffff* or *pppp*), which basically tell you to play as loud or as soft as possible.

TIP

Trumpets and violins
Some instruments sound louder than others. If a ff is indicated for a violin as well as for a trumpet, the musicians should take care that the trumpet doesn't overplay the violin, of course.

Until the next
Dynamic markings are always printed under the first note they apply to. From that note onward you keep playing at the indicated volume until you come across the next dynamic marking.

GRADUAL DYNAMIC CHANGES

There are also dynamic markings that tell you to get gradually louder (*crescendo*) or softer (*decrescendo*).

Crescendo – getting louder

Crescendo (Italian for 'growing') tells you to get gradually louder over a number of notes or bars. The sign used for short crescendos clearly indicates this: It shows two diverging lines (—————) under the notes or bars it applies to. A crescendo that's stretched over a larger number of bars is often indicated by the word 'crescendo,' or the abbreviation cresc., followed by a dotted line. The crescendo ends where that line stops.

Decrescendo – getting softer

A short decrescendo is indicated by two converging lines (—————). For long decrescendos, you'll find the full word or its abbreviation decresc. or decr., followed by the dotted line mentioned above. *Diminuendo* (dim.) is another word for decrescendo.

Reading ahead

How much louder or softer you should get is indicated by a dynamic marking at the end of the (de)crescendo — so always read ahead.

A short crescendo, from piano to forte.

Tipcode MOP-023

Wedges and hairpins

The diverging and converging (de)crescendo lines shown above are known as (de)crescendo *wedges* or *hairpins*.

53

Softer and slower

Other terms indicate that you have to get gradually softer as well
as slower, such as *smorzando* or *morendo* (die away, literally),
calando, *deficiendo*, or *perdendosi*.

Messa di voce

A *messa di voce* is a crescendo and a decrescendo on one, long note.
Vocalists use this as a (warm-up) exercise.

Tipcode MOP-057

SUDDEN DYNAMIC CHANGES

A note or chord with the marking *forzato* or *forzando* (*fz*) needs
to be accented, while *sforzando* or *sforzato* (*sfz*) indicates a strong,
sudden accent: The 's' stands for the Italian word 'subito' (at once,
immediately). *Sforzatissimo* (*sff*) and *forzatissimo* require an even
stronger, more forceful sound.

Loud, then soft

Forte-piano (*fp*) or *subito forte-piano* (*sfp*) tells you to play forte
and immediately get softer again. If you play a wind instrument
or a bowed string instrument, you can even do so on one note,
getting softer as you play it. At a *rinforzando* or *rinforzato* is either
a crescendo for a small group of notes, or a crescendo on one note.
The latter can be performed on wind instruments and bowed
strings, but not on a piano or a guitar, for example: On the latter
instruments, the tone fades away after the attack.

English

In non-classical music, dynamics are often indicated in English.
These terms, which have not been standardized, are often more
descriptive than simply 'loud' or 'soft'. A dynamic marking such
as 'screaming,' for instance, tells you to make your instrument
scream — and that's more than just playing it really loudly.

6

Fast and Slow

There are two main ways of indicating the speed or tempo of a piece of music: with a figure that states the number of beats per minute, or with one or more Italian terms. Additionally, there are all sorts of words that indicate how a piece should be played.

The most precise way of indicating the tempo of a piece is by stating the number of beats per minute (BPM), indicated with a note (the counting unit) and a number. As an example, ♩=120 tells you that the tempo is 120 quarter notes per minute. This tempo is about the same as the number of steps you take per minute at a brisk walk: It's commonly known as *march time*.

Metronome

You can set the number of beats per minute on a *metronome*, a device that will play that tempo with steady ticks or beeps. Most metronomes have a range of 40 to 208 beats per minute. Music written any slower than 40 BPM is extremely rare. For really fast pieces, you simply halve the metronome indication. If the tempo is 264 (♩ = 264), you set the metronome to 132.

Two mechanical metronomes and two electronic ones.

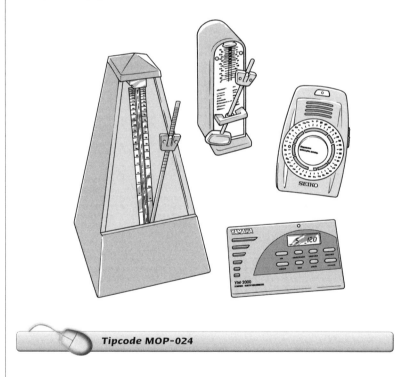

Tipcode MOP-024

Metronome types

There are both mechanical (analog) and electronic (digital) metronomes. The latter are smaller and less expensive, and they

56

usually feature various extras. Many metronomes allow you to set the time signature, for example. Tips:

- If you can set the time signature, the metronome will stress **every first beat** of the bar.

- Some metronomes can play **subdivisions**, such as sixteenth notes or triplets. Other features include an adjustable volume level, a headphone output, or an extended BPM range (say, from 10 to 300).

- Most electronic metronomes can play the note **A=440**, the reference pitch to which most bands and orchestras tune their instruments. Advanced devices offer both a metronome and an electronic tuner.

- If you are online, you can use a **virtual metronome**. Simply search for those two words, or for 'metronome online' or 'online metronome.'

- Smartphone users may download a **metronome application**, which typically has the same features as a digital metronome.

ITALIAN

Tempo can also be indicated with Italian terms. Most metronomes show the common Italian tempo markings and how they relate to the number of beats per minute. These are the main markings:

Italian	Translation	Metronome marking
Largo	very slow	♩ = 40-60
Adagio	slow	♩ = 66-76
Andante	medium slow (walking pace)	♩ = 76-108
Moderato	medium	♩ = 108-120
Allegro	fast	♩ = 120-168
Presto	very fast	♩ = 168-200

57

Prestissimo and larghetto

These tempo markings and other Italian terms often appear with different endings or suffixes. The suffix -issimo, for instance, means 'more than,' while -etto stands for 'less than'. So *prestissimo* is faster than presto, with a metronome marking of 200 to 208, and *larghetto* is a bit less slow than largo.

Rubato

The term *rubato* appears mainly in tranquil compositions. It indicates that you're free to play a few notes a bit faster, then to stretch the tempo just a bit, and so on. The expression stems from the Italian word for robbing: You 'steal' a little time from one bar or note and add it to another.

Tempo changes

Most pieces are played at the same tempo from beginning to end. While in most cases it's up to the drummer or the conductor to keep that tempo steady, it is a good idea to use a metronome when practicing, from time to time. This helps you develop your inner clock. In some pieces the tempo does change, however. One of the most common examples is when you need to slow down towards the end, in the last few bars.

Italian words

Gradual tempo changes are usually marked with Italian words too:

- *Accelerando* (think of a car's accelerator) and *stringendo* (string.; urgently) indicate that the tempo should **gradually go up**.

- If you have to **slow down**, you'll read *ritenuto* (rit. or riten.), *rallentando* (rall.), or *ritardando* (ritard.).

- *Allargando* means 'broaden out.' It can be interpreted as indicating both a crescendo and a **ritenuto**, so you get both louder and slower.

- *A tempo* tells you to return to the previous tempo.

- *Tempo I°* (tempo primo) indicates a return to the tempo **at the beginning of the piece**.

Gradually
Just as with gradual changes of volume, the words *poco a poco* (bit by bit) may be added if the change should be very gradual.

English
Of course, regular English words or phrases can be used to indicate the tempo as well, ranging from the basic 'fast' to more musical expressions such as 'slow ballad' (think 60 to 70 BPM) or 'up tempo', with some 200+ beats per minute.

TIP

M.M.

A final note: Metronome markings sometimes include the abbreviation M.M. This stands for Maelzel's Metronome. In the early nineteenth century, Johann Maelzel improved and patented the metronome, which was invented in or around 1812 by a Dutchman named Dietrich Winkel.

TEMPOS AND MOODS

If you write a song to tell the world you just won the lottery, you are likely to pick a pretty high tempo — and vice versa. The tempo often reflects the mood of a piece of music. That said, up tempo pieces do not necessarily sound sad, of course.

Feeling
There are many different, mostly Italian terms that composers use to indicate the mood or feeling of the music. Outside the classical world, you will come across similar English terms as well.

Agitato, animato	agitated
Amoroso	amorous, affectionate, loving
Appassionato	passionate
Armonioso	harmonious

59

Con brio	with brilliance
Con fuoco	with fire
Con spirito	with spirit or vigor
Dolce	sweetly, lovely
Doloroso	sad, woesome
Espressivo	expressively, dramatically
Feroce	ferocious
Gracioso	gracefully, elegantly
Grave	solemnly, seriously, slowly
Maestoso	majestically, stately
Mosso	lively, moved
Tranquillo	calmly, quietly, tranquilly
Vivace	lively

 TIP

More terms

You don't need to speak Italian to understand the meaning of most of the terms above, such as amoroso, appassionato, *or* armonioso. *The same goes for many other musical terms.* Luminoso *means luminously (brightly, shiningly),* misterioso *is Italian for mysteriously, and* ritmico *means rhythmical, of course.*

Tempo and feeling
Tempo related Italian terms often tell you how to play a piece or a section as well. Largo means slowly, but also broadly, while allegro indicates that the music should sound lively or joyful.

Sostenuto
The term *sostenuto* means sustained. If the word sostenuto (sost.) is printed above or below a note, you're supposed to sustain that note.

Very, more, or less
The words in the following list are often combined with terms already mentioned:

alla	in the [...] style (alla Turca: in the Turkish style)
assai	quite, rather, much
molto	very
meno	less
(ma) non troppo	(but) not too much
più	more
un poco	a little, a bit
e	and

A mouthful

So un poco più presto tells you to start playing a little faster. And poco a poco stringendo e crescendo ma non troppo means that you should gradually get a little faster and a bit louder as well, but please, don't overdo it.

Ad libitum

Ad libitum or *ad lib.* means 'at liberty.' These words tell you that it's up to you how you want to play a section or a piece of music. It often refers to the tempo, but it may also have a much broader meaning, or another specific meaning. An example: 8va ad lib. tells you that you can play a certain section an octave higher if you feel like it, but you don't have to.

61

7

Articulation

Just like words, you can 'pronounce' or articulate notes
in different ways. The way notes should be articulated is
indicated by a variety of symbols.

The best known articulation sign is the accent: a horizontal 'V' above or below a note. It tells you to emphasize the note, typically by playing it a little louder.

Accented notes

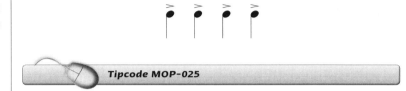

Tipcode MOP-025

Marcato

An upside-down 'V' indicates a *marcato* ('marked' or 'stressed'). Notes with this sign should be played louder, and often just bit shorter as well. If there is a dot within the marcato sign, the notes have to be even shorter. Alternatively, the word marcato can be used to indicate a group of notes or bars that should be played this way.

Marcato: stressed.

TIP

Different approaches

Other books may provide slightly different explanations of these and other terms. Likewise, the marcato sign may come with a different explanation for jazz musicians (short and accented) than for string players, for example. But in the end, it is always a matter of interpretation. The music and its context will guide you in how you should play notes with these and other articulation markings.

Staccato

Notes with a dot above or below them are to be played *staccato*:

Staccato: short notes.

Tipcode MOP-026

very short, or clipped. Remember though, a staccato quarter note *sounds* shorter than a regular quarter note, but its note value or *time value* doesn't change. The word 'staccato' may replace a number of staccato dots.

Staccatissimo

If there's a small triangle printed above or below the note, instead of a dot, the notes should be played *staccatissimo*: even shorter than staccato.

Staccatissimo: even shorter notes.

Legato

Legato (literally 'bound' or 'tied together') can be seen as the opposite of staccato. You make the notes last as long as they can, so each note flows into the next. The notes are marked with the word legato or with a curved line, the *legato slu*r. If you're a string player, you should play legato notes with the same stroke of the bow. Horn players play them in the same breath, and keyboard players hold each key down until they press the next key.

Tipcode MOP-027

Legato: The notes are smoothly bound together.

Phrase mark

The *phrase mark* looks very similar to a legato slur, but it has a different meaning. It joins a larger number of notes together in a

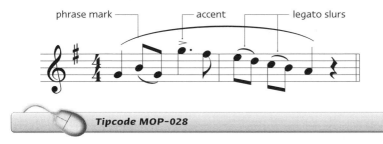

phrase mark ——— accent ——— legato slurs

Phrase mark: to be played like a phrase.

Tipcode MOP-028

65

phrase, just like words. And that's how you play them: as a phrase. Of course phrase marks may be combined with other markings, such as the legato slurs and the accents in the following example.

Tenuto

Accenting a note or a chord by holding it slightly longer (rather than playing it louder) is known as an *agogic accent*. This can be indicated with a *tenuto mark*: a dash above or below the notes. A difference between tenuto, Italian for 'held', and legato is that tenuto notes may be stressed a little.

Portato

Portato notes are typically played a little longer, but not as long as in a legato. The notes don't flow into the next notes. If regular notes are played as 'daa daa daa', and legato as 'daahaahaa', portato would be 'daadaadaa'. Portato can be indicated with a dash above or below each note, or with a slur and dots above or below the notes.

Portato: dashes or dots and a slur.

Simile

The word 'similar' stems from the Italian word *simile*. Simile tells you to continue a certain way of playing. Printed after a few staccato notes, for instance, it means that all the notes that follow are to be played staccato too.

Fermata or pause

A *fermata* is a note, chord, or rest that is prolonged until the conductor, the band leader or the drummer puts an end to it, or, if you're playing solo, until you are done with it. You usually find a fermata or pause at the end of a piece, but it can be used to mark the end of a musical phrase or a section as well. The fermata or *pause sign* is a dot within a curved line.

Fermata: a suspension of time.

fermata

Pizzicato and col legno

There are many other markings that tell you how to play certain notes. Some of these markings apply to specific instruments only. *Pizzicato*, for example, tells orchestral string players to pluck their strings rather than to use their bow (*arco*, *archetto*). The words *col legno* (with wood) tell them to hit (*battuto*) or bow (*tratto*) the strings with the wooden stick of their bow, instead of with the bow hair.

Arpeggio

An *arpeggio* can be played on keyboard instruments, guitars, and other chord instruments. It tells you to play the notes of a chord as if you play a harp, in a rapid succession, rather than at the same time.

Arpeggio.

Tipcode MOP-029

JAZZ

Various markings are used in certain musical styles only. In jazz and related styles you may come across the scoop, the du-wah, and ghost notes, for example. These markings are sometimes referred to as *ornaments* (see Chapter 8).

Scoop

A *scoop* tells you to briefly bend the pitch of a note down-ward, not more than a half step. Scoops are most commonly found in sax parts.

A scoop.

Du and wah

The *du-wah* is used mainly by brass players. The 'du' (a plus sign above the note) tells you to smother the sound by putting

67

your hand or a plunger (a type of mute) in front of the bell of the instrument. The 'wah' (a small circle) tells you to open up the bell again. Harmonica players du-wah with their hands, and a guitarist's wah-wah pedal produces a similar effect: Technically speaking, it alters the harmonic content of the sound, reducing and/or boosting certain harmonics or overtones.

Smothered and open: du-wah du-wah.

Ghost notes

A *ghost note* is a dead-sounding, 'swallowed' note with a hardly definable pitch. Every instrument requires a specific technique to produce these notes. Wind players use their tongue, guitarists muffle the string they're playing, and so on. Drummers play ghost notes as soft taps on the snare drum, between the other beats.

Ghost note: dead-sounding.

TIP

Breath marks

Singers and horn players may find breath marks in their charts. A small comma tells you to take a short breath, while a V or a tick typically indicates that you have more time to breathe. If no such signs are present, you may include them yourself, as many musicians do. The same comma is also used for string players, who have to lift the bow at that point.

68

8

Ornaments

In music, ornaments are decorative notes that embellish the main notes. This chapter introduces the most common ones, from trills to turns, and shows you how to play them. The exact rhythm of each, though, can change depending on tempo and taste.

There are dozens of ornaments, divided into a few large families. The shake family, for example, includes the trill, the mordent, and the vibrato, among others; the ornaments in the appoggiatura family all have an accessory note added to the main note; the division family divides a note into a few shorter ones.

Tipcode MOP-030

Trill

Perhaps the best-known ornament is the *trill*, played by rapidly alternating between the *main note* or *principal note* and the next higher note in the key signature, referred to as the *upper note*. A trill or *shake* can begin either on the principal note or on the upper note. A trill is usually indicated by the abbreviation tr.

Trill.

Mordent

There are two types of mini-trills, known as *mordents*. The *regular mordent* or *lower mordent* is a very rapid trill with the note one step below. It is also known as a *open shake*.

Mordent: short trill to the lower note.

Inverted mordent

The *inverted mordent* or *upper mordent* is a similar trill with the note one step up. This mordent is also known as a Prall trill. The

Upper or inverted mordent.

only visible difference between the symbols for the lower and the upper mordent is that the lower mordent has a small vertical line.

Sharps, flats, and trills

Trills and mordents are played on the note above or below the principal note in the key signature that you're in: Sharps and flats remain valid. If the figure is to include a note that's not in the key signature, a flat, sharp, or natural sign will make this clear.

Written   Played

Mordent with a temporarily lowered E (E♭).

Double trill

A *double trill* is a rapid alternation between two main notes and two other notes, usually a third higher.

Written   Played

A double trill.

Tremolo

A *tremolo* is a quick repetition of one note. On brass wind instruments you can play a tremolo on one note by making a r-r-rolling 'r' with your tongue. In classical music this is called *flutter tonguing* or — in German — *Flatterzunge*; jazz musicians speak of *growling*.

Written   Played

Tremolo on one note.

More on tremolo

A tremolo may also indicate a rapid alternation between two notes that are a third or more apart. Outside of the classical world the

71

term is used to indicate rapid variations in the output volume of an electric or electronic instrument (*volume modulation*).

Vibrato

A *vibrato* is a repeated, very slight *pitch fluctuation* or *pitch modulation*, (much) less than a half step. On fretted instruments (e.g., guitars) and string instruments, you play a vibrato by subtly rocking the finger that stops the string. Wind players use their embouchure (the muscles in and around the mouth) and air stream control, and electronic keyboard players have a vibrato control at the left hand.

No symbol

You may find the word *vibrato* (vib., vibr.) under a note, but the use of vibrato is commonly up to the player or the conductor — unless the composer specifies *non-vibr.*

Acciaccaturas

An *acciaccatura* is a small auxiliary note that can be played on the beat, before the beat, or, very briefly, simultaneously with the main note. It is indicated as an eighth note in small type, with a strike across its stem.

Acciaccatura.

Written   Played

Appoggiaturas

The *appoggiatura* is a similar ornamental note, yet without the strike. Other than the acciaccatura, it is often said to have a set length, usually taking up half of the length of the main note. If it precedes a dotted note, it takes up the length of the note without the dot.

Grace note?

Experts disagree whether an acciaccatura is a *grace note*, a term that some explicitly reserve for the appoggiatura. Others refer to the appoggiatura as a long, 'leaning' grace note, defining the acciaccatura as a short, 'crushed' grace note.

Schleifer

A *Schleifer* is an ornament from the Baroque. It's a brief slide that takes you to the main note. It is usually started on the beat.

or

A Schleifer.

Turn

A *turn* or *gruppetto* ('division') tells you to play around the principal note. The symbol clearly shows what it is supposed to sound like.

Written   Played

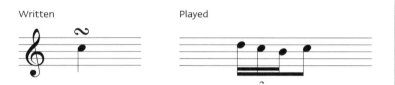

Turn: playing around the principal note.

The other way around

A *reversed turn*, simply indicated by a reversed turn symbol, tells you to play the notes the other way around. In this example, you'd play B C D C instead of D C B C.

The turn between two notes

You may also come across turn symbols between two notes. This ornament joins up the notes, as it were.

Written   Played

3

Three extra notes between two main notes.

Glissando

A *glissando* is a slide from one note to another. The way to play it varies per instrument. On a trombone you use the slide, of course; on a keyboard instrument you sweep your fingertips over the keys; on fretted instruments and string instruments you slide your fingers over the strings. Many electronic keyboard instruments have a pitch bend control, allowing you to bend a note up or

73

down. A *slide* can be seen as a very short glissando; it's actually an appoggiatura with two accessory notes.

Glissando: sliding from note to note.

Fall, lift, plop, and doit
A glissando always indicates a first and a last note. *Falls, lifts, plops,* and *doits* don't. Their symbols show you quite clearly how they should be played. The exact execution is up to you or your musical director.

Fall: Falling down from the note.

Lift: Move up from the note.

Plop: Falling into the note, from above.

Doit: a short upward bend of the note.

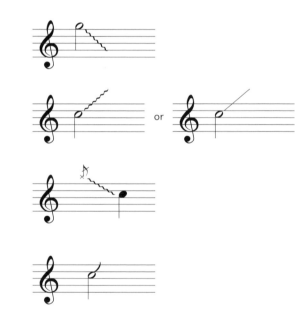

9

Repeat Signs and Navigation Markers

Compositions usually consist of a number of different sections, such as the verses and choruses that make up most songs. Often, these sections will be repeated once or a number of times, or your chart will tell you to go backwards or forwards to a particular point in the music. There are special markings that direct you around a piece of music, as well as a number of repeat signs that indicate the repetition of a note or one or more bars.

Reading a chart becomes a lot easier if you know that compositions always have a certain form. Even the simplest of songs, such as 'Twinkle, Twinkle'. It has twelve bars, and the melody of the first four bars is exactly the same as the melody of the last four bars; the four bars in the middle are different.

In letters

If you'd assign the letter A to the melody of the first four bars, and a B to the middle four, 'Twinkle, Twinkle' has the form ABA: The last four bars are identical to the first four.

Choruses and verses

Pop songs, lullabies and numerous other types of songs typically consist of a number of *verses* and a *chorus*. Each verse has the same melody but different lyrics, while the chorus is a section that is repeated throughout the song without changes in melody or lyrics.

Intro and outro

Many songs start with an *intro*, typically a number of instrumental bars before the vocals come in — but there are vocal intros as well. The *outro* refers to the final section of a song, which may also be referred to as the *coda* (the 'tail' of the piece, literally).

Bridge

A *bridge* is another section of a song. The melody and lyrics are different from the chorus or the verse, and bridges are often in another key as well (modulation; see page 98).

Section markings

In larger compositions, letters are also used to indicate the sections of the piece. These *section markings* are also known as *rehearsal marks*, as that's how they're often used: Instead of playing a piece from the top after every mistake, the conductor may suggest to 'take it from H', for example. These markings are usually printed in small boxes above the staff.

Bar numbers

Instead, *bar numbers* may be used. These numbers are printed above the bar line that marks the beginning of the relevant bar.

Not every bar is numbered; they're often printed at the first bar of each staff only.

intro · C · 25 · chorus

section line

Names, letters, or numbers are used to identify the various parts of a piece.

Classical music

Classical compositions often consist of various parts or movements that each have their own form. For example, a symphony, an extended work for orchestra, often starts with an *allegro* (the opening *sonata*), followed by a slower movement (*adagio*), a faster *minuet* or (in later days) a *scherzo*, with an *allegro* (fast) movement at the end. There are many other terms that describe sections in classical works, such as *exposition* (an opening section), *recapitulation* (a return to the opening), and *interlude* or *transition* (an interplay or 'classical bridge' that connects two other sections). If you're about to start playing a new piece, ask your teacher or the conductor to explain its form.

REPEAT SIGNS

Repeat signs tell you to repeat one or more bars, or a section of the piece.

Repeat signs for one and two bars.

One and two bars

The repeat sign for a single bar is a slash with a dot on either side. A similar symbol with two slashes tells you to repeat the two preceding bars. These symbols are known as *simile marks*.

77

More bars

A section that should be played twice is usually marked with two repeat signs, one at either end of the section. The illustration below shows you what this looks like. When you reach the second repeat sign (its two dots facing 'backward'), you go back to the first sign (its dots facing 'forward') and play again from there, repeating what you just played.

Repeat the bars between these two signs.

Just one sign

If you have to repeat the first section of a piece, there may be just one repeat sign (the 'second' one, its dots facing to the left). When you reach this sign, go back to the beginning of the piece and play the entire section once more.

Repeat from the beginning.

First and second ending

A repeated section may end differently the second time around, creating a bridge to the following section. This is indicated with square brackets marked 1 and 2, as in the example below. You end the section the first time around by playing the bar or bars marked 1 (the *first ending*). When you get to this point the second time, you go to the bar or bars marked 2 (*second ending*). In Italian the first and second ending are known as *prima volta* (*Ima volta*) and *seconda volta* (*IIda volta*) respectively.

First and second ending.

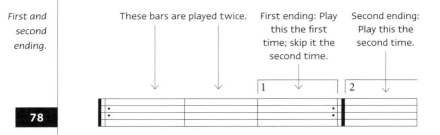

These bars are played twice. First ending: Play this the first time; skip it the second time. Second ending: Play this the second time.

Three or more

If you need to play the first section not twice, but three or more times, it will be marked 1, 2, 3 (etc.). The consecutive number will be under the second bracket.

On cue

In jazz and other styles of music, it may be up to the soloist how often a certain section is repeated. This may be marked as *on cue* or *on Q*.

REPEATING NOTES AND CHORDS

The following signs tell you to repeat single chords, single notes, and pairs of alternating notes.

Repeating chords

If a chord is followed by a slash or series of slashes, you should repeat the chord once for each slash.

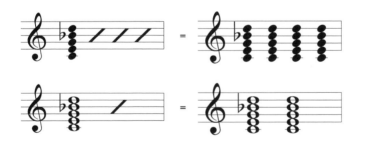

Repeat the chord once for each slash.

Just slashes

In pop, jazz and other styles of music, you may find charts that show no more than a slash for each beat. Chord symbols (see page 154) printed above the staff indicate which chords to play on those beats. The exact rhythm of the chords is up to the player or the band leader.

TIP

79

Repeating notes

A single note with one or more slashes tells you to repeat the note. The slashes have the same value as flags or beams: one slash tells you to play eighth notes, two slashes indicate sixteenths, and so on. In 4/4, a whole note with a single slash above it tells you to play eighth notes for four beats. Two more examples:

Different pitch

A repetition of alternating notes of different pitches can be indicated in a similar way.

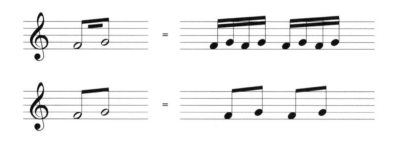

NAVIGATION MARKERS

A variety of symbols, words, and abbreviations is used to indicate that you have to go from one part of a piece to another.

Da Capo

Da Capo (D.C.) means that you go back to the beginning (capo) of a piece and repeat everything you played so far. When you reach D.C. the second time, ignore it and continue with the music that follows. Basically, Da Capo means the same as the single repeat sign explained on page 78.

Dal Segno

Dal Segno (D.S.) means 'from the sign.' When you reach a D.S., you go back to the 𝄉 sign (the segno), which always precedes the D.S. marking. You repeat the bars between the segno and the D.S. once, and ignore D.S. the second time you reach it.

Al Coda

You may have to move around even more. A common example: *Da Capo Al Coda* means you have to go back to the beginning of the piece (D.C.), and play until you reach the coda sign ⊕. This sign tells you to go to the coda, a section at the end of the piece (the *tail piece*). This section is marked with the word coda or — again — the coda sign ⊕. (Check out the example on page 82).

To the coda

Al coda is Italian for 'to the coda.' Instead of those exact words, you may also find the abbreviation Al ⊕.

Other combinations

Coda markings can be combined with other instructions. Dal Segno al ⊕, for example, tells you to go back to the 𝄉 sign, play on until you reach the ⊕ sign, and then go to the coda.

Complex

If you're playing a piece with a complicated form, numerous repeats and other signposts, you may jot the basic form down. This will help you understand the music, and it possibly saves you from having to look for segnos, repeat signs and other markings onstage.

Fine

Al Fine means 'to the end'. Da Capo al Fine (or D.C. al Fine) means go back to the beginning, and then finish the piece where the word Fine is printed. The Italian word 'fine' is pronounced as 'feenah'.

Example

Here's an example of a piece of music with various repeat and section markings.

1. Play the first seven bars plus the one under the first ending (Section A, first time).

2. Repeat the first seven bars and play the bar under the second ending (Section A, second time).

3. Play Section B.

4. Go back to the beginning at D.C. al Coda.

5. From the Coda sign (Section A, seventh bar) you go to the Coda.

6. The double bar line at the end of the coda is the end of the piece.

AABA form with various repeat and section markings.

The sign or the word

In this example, the coda sign $\oplus$ is used to tell you to go to the coda at the end of the piece, marked with the word coda. You may also find the reverse (the words al coda replacing the initial sign and the sign itself marking the coda), or composers may use the coda sign twice, for example.

The form

The 'song' on the previous page has the form AABA: The first eight bars are played twice (AA), followed by eight different bars (B) and ending with the first eight (A). This form is used for numerous musical songs and jazz standards.

Rhythm changes

Well known examples include jazz standards such as *Anthropology* (Charlie Parker and Dizzy Gillespie), *Oleo* (Sonny Rollins), or the George Gershwin composition *I've Got Rhythm*. Based on that title, these forms are known as *rhythm changes*. If you don't know any of these melodies, please listen to them through YouTube or a similar online source, or sing the tune of the famous 1960s television series, *The Flintstones*. Count the bars as you listen, and you will definitely recognize the AABA form.

More forms

There are many different forms, of course. Pop songs may have a form such as chorus, verse, chorus, verse, chorus, bridge, chorus, but they can start with two verses as well, for example.

Letters

As each verse has its own lyrics, the verses are often numbered. The song in the paragraph above would then look like A B1 A B2 A C A, which is a lot easier to the eye. The A's are the choruses, B1 and B2 the verses, and C is the bridge. The figures may be replaced by accents: A B A B', etc.

Classical music

In classical music, similar forms or structures can be found. A *Viennese rondo*, for example, has the form A B A C A B A coda. Accents mark variations on earlier sections with the same letter.

83

10

Major and Minor

If you play all the natural notes from C to C, you're playing a scale: C D E F G A B C. Do the same from A to A, and you will hear a scale that clearly sounds different. You may wonder why, as you're using the exact same keys. The answer is simple: If you start playing the white keys on a different key, the order of whole and half steps changes, turning it into a completely different scale.

Most compositions are based on the notes that belong to one particular scale. The name of that scale is referred to as the *key* of the composition. This chapter deals with the two most important scales: major and minor.

A lot easier

It's not essential to know about scales and keys in order to read music — but it does help you to understand what you're playing, instead of just playing the notes one by one, with no sense of their function in the context of the music. It definitely makes improvising and writing your own music a lot easier too.

In a row

Pick any tune and arrange all its notes in a row, from low to high. What you will end up with is a scale, or part of a scale. 'Twinkle, Twinkle,' for example, is made up of the notes C, G, A, G, F, E, D, C. Arranged from low to high (C, D, E, F, G, A), they are the first six notes of a scale.

Root

If you sing 'Twinkle, Twinkle' and stop at the words 'what you,' it probably feels like you're ending it in mid-flight: There's got to be more to come. The note you're missing is the *root note* or, simply, the *root*. This last note makes you go back to where it all started: to the root of the piece. The root is usually the first note of the scale that has been used for a piece of music.

'Twinkle, Twinkle.' The root is C.

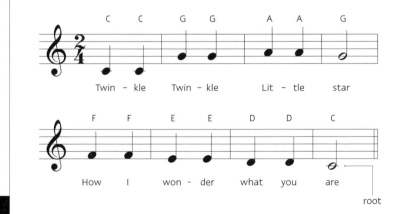

Coming home

Most pieces end on the root of the scale in which they are written. Another term for root, clearly indicating this function, is *home note*. It's also known as the *tonic* or the *key note*.

The scale of C

'Twinkle, Twinkle,' on the previous page, is made up of the first six notes of the scale of C. To complete the scale, just add the B and a second C: What you get is C D E F G A B C. On a keyboard, you'll see that this scale is made up of natural (white) notes only.

Whole steps and half steps

If you go from one white key to the next on a keyboard, you're playing a mixture of whole and half steps, as shown on the keyboard below. From C to D and from D to E are whole steps. From E to F is a half step, for example.

The difference

The difference between whole and half steps is easier to see than it may be to hear, at first, so take another look at the piano keyboard. There is no black key between the white notes E and F, so from E to F is a half step. The same is true when you go from the white note B to the white note C.

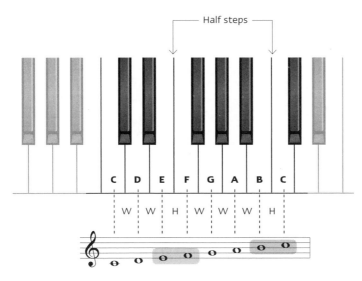

The scale of C. The two half steps are from E to F, and from B to C.

Major scale

The scale on the previous page consists of seven steps. There are five whole steps (W) and two half steps (H), in the following order: W W H W W W H. This order means that it's a major scale.

Different order, different sound

If you change the order of whole and half steps, you'll end up with a different scale. This new scale has a different character due to the altered order of whole and half steps.

A circle

Drawing the W and H steps in a circle clearly demonstrates this. First follow the steps in the circle starting on C (the root), going round clockwise. You'll see the whole and half steps coming by in the order mentioned above: It's a major scale.

The roots of the C-major and A-minor scales. Follow the arrows and you will see the different orders of the steps for these scales.

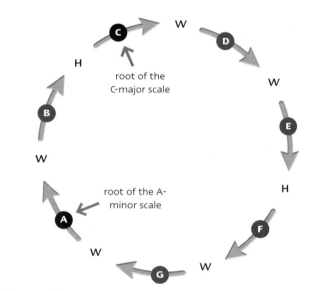

Another note

If you start on another note, you'll get a different order of the whole and half steps. The result is a different scale.

Minor scale

If you have a keyboard instrument at hand, you can easily hear that difference. First, listen to the scale that you get when you

88

play the white keys from C to the next higher C. Then move your hand a little to the left and play the white notes from A to the next higher A. The second scale sounds a little lower, but it also sounds a bit sadder or darker than the major scale. This scale is known as the *minor scale*. You play the same white keys, but the scale sounds different because the order of whole and half steps is different: W H W W H W W.

New order

In the minor scale, the half steps are on positions two and five, rather than three and seven, which makes for a completely different sound.

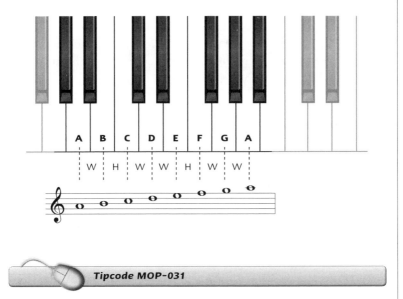

The minor scale, from A to A: W H W W H W W.

Tipcode MOP-031

Blocks

If you draw the steps of the major and minor scales as a series of whole and half-sized blocks, as shown on the next page, you will immediately see how different they look — and things that look different, usually sound different too.

Keys and scales

Scales are named after their root note. The major scale with the

89

root C is the *C major scale*. A piece of music that uses these notes is in the key of *C major*.

The major and minor scales have different outlines.

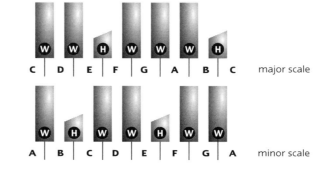

major scale

minor scale

More scales

Each time you start the circle on page 88 on another note, you will a new scale: The seven white notes allow for seven different scales. This chapter covers two of them: the major scale and the minor scale. The other five follow in Chapter 14.

> ## Minor is sad?
>
> If you listen to a major scale followed by a minor scale, you won't be surprised that minor scales are often said to have a 'sad' character. Still, there are cheerful songs in a minor scale and sad, moving songs that are based on a major scale.

MAJOR SCALES

A major scale can start on C or any other note. All you have to do is make sure that the order of the steps remains the same as in C major: W W H W W W H. This sounds harder than it is.

The order of the steps

In Chapter 4, you already found that you can begin 'Twinkle, Twinkle' on C, but also on F or D. In order to make it sound like

'Twinkle, Twinkle,' one note had to be lowered when starting the song on F. When played in D instead, one note had to be raised. In other words: You raised or lowered notes to maintain the desired tonal distances. With scales, it's just the same.

From F to F

If you play the white keys from F to F, for example, the order of whole and half steps is W W W H W W H. No keyboard at hand? Then check the circle on page 88. This order does not correspond with the order of the major scale: The first half step has moved from the third to the fourth position. You can hear the difference, and you can clearly see the difference below.

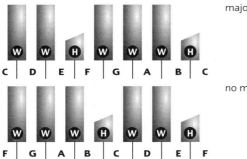

major scale

no major scale

The steps from C to C and from F to F, played on the white keys only; the difference is obvious. From F to F is not a major scale: The order of Ws and Hs is different.

F major in blocks

To play a major scale starting on F, all you have to do is change the

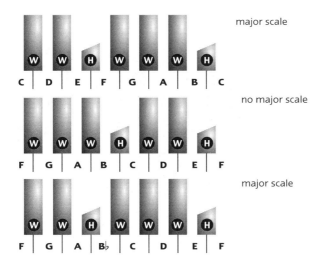

major scale

no major scale

major scale

Turning a B into a B♭ corrects the order of the steps in this scale.

91

order of whole and half steps. You do so, in this case, by lowering the B. This turns it into B♭. As a result, you get the 'major' order of whole and half steps, starting on F: the F major scale!

On the keyboard

The two keyboard examples below show the difference between playing all the white notes from F to F (no major scale), and lowering the B, which turns it into a major scale.

Lowering the B to a B♭ turns this sequence into a F-major scale.

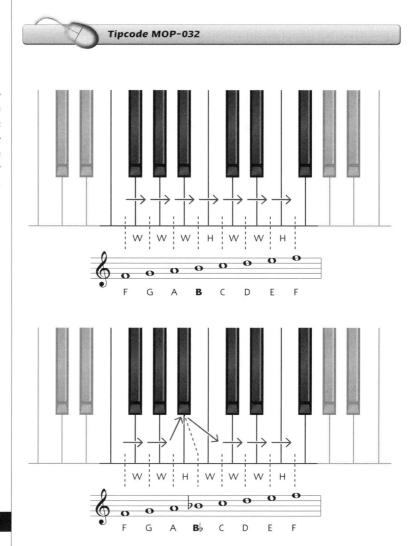

G major

In the example above, a flat was added. If you start a scale on other notes, you may need more flats or one or more sharps to turn it into a major scale. If, for example, you go from G to the next higher G on the white keys, you will find that the order of the last two steps differs from that of the major scale: it's H W instead of W H.

An F with a sharp

In other words, things go wrong from E to F and from F to G, as you can see below. The solution is to raise or sharpen the F. This will automatically turn the last two steps into a whole and a half one. The result is the scale of G major!

The natural notes from G. The order of the last two steps (H, W) does not correspond with the major scale: it should be W, H.

The scale of G-major: The F has been raised.

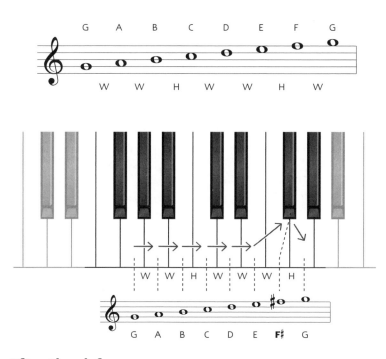

After the clef

If a piece is written in G major, you won't find a sharp in front of every F. Instead, there's a single sharp at the clef. That one sharp is the *key signature* of the piece (see pages 45–47). It turns all Fs in the piece into F♯s.

93

More than one

Most key signatures have more than one flat or sharp. Here's one with three flats, as an example. To get the whole and half steps in the scale of E♭ major in the right order, three notes have to be lowered, so the key signature has three flats: B♭, E♭, and A♭.

The scale of E♭-major, with three flats.

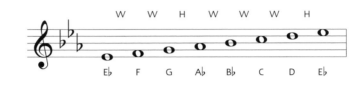

The major scales

Every major scale has its own key signature, with a set number of sharps or flats. The following table shows the flats and sharps for each key signature, and it tells you which notes are raised or lowered. Page 211 shows the major scales on a staff.

Sharps and flats in major scales.

MAJOR SCALES

Key signature	Tonic	Sharps and flats	
C-major	C	0	
G-major	G	1 ♯	F♯
D-major	D	2 ♯♯	F♯, C♯
A-major	A	3 ♯♯ ♯	F♯, C♯, G♯
E-major	E	4 ♯♯ ♯♯	F♯, C♯, G♯, D♯
B-major	B	5 ♯♯ ♯♯ ♯	F♯, C♯, G♯, D♯, A♯
F♯-major	F♯	6 ♯♯ ♯♯ ♯♯	F♯, C♯, G♯, D♯, A♯, E♯
G♭-major	G♭	6 ♭♭ ♭♭ ♭♭	B♭, E♭, A♭, D♭, G♭, C♭
D♭-major	D♭	5 ♭♭ ♭♭ ♭	B♭, E♭, A♭, D♭, G♭
A♭-major	A♭	4 ♭♭ ♭♭	B♭, E♭, A♭, D♭
E♭-major	E♭	3 ♭♭ ♭	B♭, E♭, A♭
B♭-major	B♭	2 ♭♭	B♭, E♭
F-major	F	1 ♭	B♭

Always the same

As you may remember from page 46, the sharps and flats 'appear in a fixed order': The sharps and flats in a key signature always refer to the same notes. If there's just one sharp, it raises every F to an F♯. If the key signature shows two sharps, every C is raised as well — and so on.

Go Down
The following mnemonic helps you remember the number of sharps in the major scales: **G**o **D**own **A**nd **E**at **B**reakfast **F**irst: G has one sharp, D has two, etc. (For the number of flats, reverse the order: F has one flat, B♭ had two, and so on.)

The number tells it all
Likewise, one flat turns every B into a B♭; the second flat lowers every E too, the third also lowers every A, and so on. The number of sharps or flats in the key signature tells you right away which notes to raise or lower.

Enharmonic scales
The following is good to know:

- *The table on page 94 lists two scales that sound identical: The scales of F♯ and G♭ are **enharmonic scales** (page 105).*

- *There are scales with more than six flats or sharps. C♭ major, for example, has **seven flats**. Page 105 tells you why you hardly even see such scales.*

Not so difficult
A piece with four or five sharps or flats looks more complicated than it is. With a bit of practice and talent, you'll find that you will play the right notes almost automatically. Once you've grasped the system underlying the order of the sharps and flats, things become even easier. This system is covered in the next chapter.

One tone
If the order of the whole and half steps in all those major scales is always the same, then why isn't everything written in C major? Wouldn't it be easier without all those sharps and flats? Yes, it would. But it would also make things pretty monotonous, which literally means 'one tone'.

95

A little different

Besides, a piece in F major not only sounds higher or lower than the same piece in C major, it also sounds a little different. That is because each key, like each color, has a certain character. Composers often deliberately choose a certain scale for a certain piece.

MINOR SCALES

The previous section basically applies to minor scales as well.

From A to A: A minor

If you play all the natural notes from one A to the next, the whole steps and half steps will be in the following order: W H W W H W W. This is the scale of A minor.

The scale of A-minor.

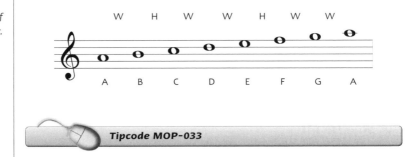

Tipcode MOP-033

C minor

If you want to play a minor scale starting on C, you will have to lower three notes: B, E, and A. When you do, you'll be playing the scale of C minor.

C-minor has three flats (B♭, E♭, and A♭).

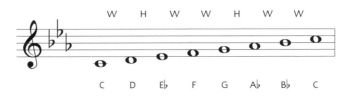

Three lowered notes

These three lowered notes are the third, the sixth, and the seventh of the scale. This is often shown as 1 2 ♭3 4 5 ♭6 ♭7. In the scale of C, those lowered notes would be the E (3), the A (6), and the B (7), as noted earlier.

The lowered third

The main difference between minor and major is in the lower lowered third note in the minor scale. To hear this difference, play the major chord C–E–G followed by the minor chord C– E♭– G. The first chord sounds bright and clear; the second sounds quite dark, sad, or melancholic.

Tipcode MOP-034

MINOR SCALES

Key signature	Tonic	Sharps and flats	
A-minor	A	0	
E-minor	E	1 ♯	F♯,
B-minor	B	2 ♯♯	F♯, C♯
F♯-minor	F♯	3 ♯♯♯	F♯, C♯, G♯
C♯-minor	C♯	4 ♯♯ ♯♯	F♯, C♯, G♯, D♯
G♯-minor	G♯	5 ♯♯ ♯♯ ♯	F♯, C♯, G♯, D♯, A♯
D♯-minor	D♯	6 ♯♯ ♯♯ ♯♯	F♯, C♯, G♯, D♯, A♯, E♯
E♭-minor	E♭	6 ♭♭ ♭♭ ♭♭	B♭, E♭, A♭, D♭, G♭, C♭
B♭-minor	B♭	5 ♭♭ ♭♭ ♭	B♭, E♭, A♭, D♭, G♭
F-minor	F	4 ♭♭ ♭♭	B♭, E♭, A♭, D♭
C-minor	C	3 ♭♭ ♭	B♭, E♭, A♭
G-minor	G	2 ♭♭	B♭, E♭
D-minor	D	1 ♭	B♭

Sharps and flats in minor scales.

The same order

As you can see above, the sharps and flats appear in the same order as they do in major scales (see page 94)!

Enharmonic scales

Note that the two scales in the middle of this table (D♯ minor and

E♭ minor) are enharmonically equivalent, just like the two scales in the middle of the table on 94.

Natural minor
The basic minor scale or mode in this chapter is also known as *natural minor, original minor,* or *pure minor.* This sets it apart from two minor modes that were derived from it. These two modes, *melodic minor* and *harmonic minor,* are covered on pages 119–121.

Scale wheel
The scale wheel on page 208 is a handy device to find the notes of the major and minor scales. It also clearly demonstrates that the order of whole and half steps is the same in any major scale — and the same goes for minor scales, of course.

OTHER NOTES

Most pieces are based on the notes of one particular scale — but that doesn't mean that all notes in a piece belong to that scale. You may very well come across accidental sharps or flats in a piece in C major or A minor; both key signatures are without sharps or flats.

Modulation
In some pieces, the music changes key. This is known as a modulation. A piece that modulates starts in one key, changes to another key at one point (you may even go through more key changes), and then usually ends in the original key. As stated on page 76, the bridge in a pop song is often in a different key than the rest of the song.

Key signature
If a piece modulates, the key signature doesn't necessarily change: Any extra sharps, flats, or natural signs can be written as accidentals. In other pieces, each new key signature is preceded by a section line.

Minor? Major!

If a piece in a minor scale (using a minor third) ends with a major chord, the major third in that chord is known as a Picardian third.

TIP

99

11

The Circle of Fifths

The fixed order of the sharps and flats is not coincidental. There's a system behind it. The circle of fifths, which is based on that system, shows you at a glance how many sharps or flats there are in a given scale.

In the previous chapter, you saw that C major has no sharps or flats. G major has one sharp (F♯). D major has two (F♯, C♯), A major has three (F♯, C♯, G♯) — and so on.

A fifth higher

If you go from the root of the major scale without sharps (C) to the root of the major scale with one sharp (G), you'll count five white notes. This tonal distance or *interval* is known as a *fifth*: G is a fifth higher than C (C=1, D=2, E=3, F=4, G=5).

Another fifth up

If you go from G to the root of the scale with two sharps (D), you go up another fifth. And from D to A (three sharps) is a fifth too. In other words, a sharp is added for every major scale that starts a fifth higher.

```
C  D  E  F  G  A  B  C
         G  A  B  C  D  E  F♯ G
                  D  E  F♯ G  A  B  C♯ D
```

The raised seventh

There's yet another pattern. Every time you go a fifth up for the next major scale, the added sharp raises the *seventh step* or degree of that new scale. The F♯ is the seventh step of the scale of G. C♯ is the seventh note of the scale of D — and so on.

Hearing it

You can hear this too. First play the white notes from C to the next higher C (C major scale). Now play the white notes from G to G: The seventh step (F) is too low. Raise it to F♯ and you're playing a major scale again (i.e., G major).

FLATS: A FIFTH LOWER

Scales with one or more flats have similar patterns. To find the next scale, you start a fifth lower: C major has no flats. F major (a fifth

lower) has one flat. B♭ major (again a fifth lower) has two flats —
and so on.

```
                        C  D  E  F  G  A  B  C
               F  G  A  B♭ C  D  E  F  G
      B♭ C  D  E♭ F  G  A  B♭
```

The lowered fourth step

The 'new' flat of the next scale always lowers the *fourth step* of that
scale: B♭ is the fourth step of the scale of F; E♭ is the fourth step of
the scale of B♭ — and so on.

CIRCLE OF FIFTHS

The circle of fifths is a very handy tool that shows you all major
scales. If you start at C and go round clockwise, you will see that

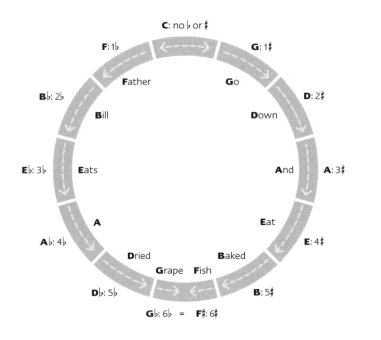

*The circle of
fifths with
all the major
scales.*

a sharp is added in every succeeding scale. Go around counter-clockwise, and a flat is added each time.

Like a clock

Just like a clock, the circle of fifths is divided into twelve. There are five minutes between the numbers on the face of a clock. Likewise, there's always a distance of five steps (a fifth) from one scale to the other. Go one fifth clockwise, from the top, and a sharp is added. Go one fifth counterclockwise, and a flat is added.

Memory joggers

Memory joggers can help you remember the number of flats and sharps for each major scale.

- Major scales with **sharps**: The scale of G major has one sharp, D major has two, and so on: Go (1) Down (2) And (3) Eat (4) Baked (5) Fish (F♯: 6 sharps).

- Major scales with **flats**: F major has one flat, B♭ has two, E♭ has three, and so on: Father (1) Bill (2) Eats (3) A (4) Dried (5) Grape (G♭: 6 flats).

Father Charles

Another memory aid helps you with the order of the sharps and flats. The sharps show up in the following order: **F**ather **C**harles **G**oes **D**own **A**nd **E**nds **B**attle (F♯, C♯, G♯, D♯, A♯, E♯, B♯. In other words, one sharp turns each F into an F♯; the second sharp tells you to play a C♯ for every C as well — and so on.

Battle Ends

The same line in reverse order tells you which notes to lower for any number of flats: **B**attle **E**nds **A**nd **D**own **G**oes **C**harles' **F**ather (B♭, E♭ A♭, D♭, G♭, C♭, F♭).

TIP

Funny cows

Instead of having Father Charles go down, you may prefer Funny Cows Go Dancing At Emily's Barn, for example — though this one doesn't work backwards.

104

Enharmonics

The six o' clock position in the circle of fifths shows G♭ major with six flats and F♯ major with six sharps. These scales and their key signatures look different, but they sound exactly the same: G♭ major and F♯ major are *enharmonic scales* (see page 48). Likewise, a piece in seven flats would sound exactly the same as the same piece in five sharps. This explains why you'll only very rarely see signatures with seven flats or sharps: You can always do with less.

The minor scales

The circle of fifths can also accommodate the minor scales, as shown on page 123.

12

Intervals

Previous chapters introduced the octave and the fifth as names for 'musical distances' from one note to another. In music, these distances are known as intervals. Knowledge of intervals isn't required to play — but it is essential if you want to understand music.

Like scales, intervals have their own character. Try playing a C and a G together, followed by a C and an F♯. The first combination sounds fine, the second one sounds less agreeable. One of the main effects of these different sounds is that they add an element of tension and release to the music.

Second, third, fourth, fifth

G is the fifth step (the fifth note) in the scale of C major. The name of this interval (C–G) is a *fifth*. The names of most intervals are based on the steps or degrees in a major scale. From C to D is a second, from C to E a third, and so on.

In every scale

It's just the same in other scales: from F to G is a second; from F to A is a third, and so on. To keep things simple, the scale of C major is used in most examples in this chapter.

Unison

If C to D is a second, the 'distance' from C to that same C is supposed to have a name too, and it has. It is known as a *unison*, which literally means 'one sound.'

Octave

The octave is the eighth step (e.g., from C to the next higher C, or from A to the next A: eight white notes). The word octave comes from the Latin word octo, which means eight (an octopus is a squid with eight arms).

Intervals between C and the notes of C-major.

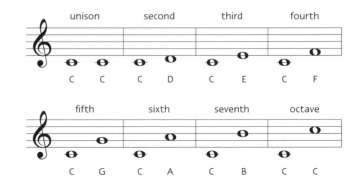

On the staff

The previous page shows the eight basic intervals of the C major scale on a staff.

> **Tipcode MOP-035**

PERFECT AND MAJOR

The eight basic intervals are divided into perfect intervals and major intervals.

Perfect intervals

Four intervals are known as the *perfect intervals*: They have an almost 'perfect', pure sound. The perfect intervals are the unison (C–C), the fourth (C–F), the fifth (C–G), and the octave (C–C). When you play each pair of notes, you'll find that the seem to fuse together — especially the octave, which tends to sound like one note only.

> **Tipcode MOP-036**

Major intervals

The other four intervals are known as *major intervals*; the second (C–D), the third (C–E), the sixth (C–A), and the seventh (C–B). If you play them, you'll hear that they sound noticeably different from the perfect intervals. Especially the second and the seventh, which sound much less 'perfect' than the perfect intervals. The third and the sixth are somewhere in between.

> **Tipcode MOP-037**

109

MINOR, DIMINISHED, AUGMENTED

The distance from C to G is a fifth. From C to A is a sixth. But you can also go from C to G♯ or G♭, for example. Here's how you name these 'in-between' intervals.

Perfect, diminished, and augmented

• Reducing a perfect interval by a half step turns it into a **diminished** interval: C–G♭ is a diminished fifth.

• Enlarging a perfect interval by a half step turns it into an **augmented** interval: C–G♯ is an augmented fifth.

diminished ⟵ *reduce* — **perfect** — *enlarge* ⟶ **augmented**

Major, minor, and augmented

• Reducing a major interval by a half step turns it into a **minor** interval: C–A♭ is a minor sixth.

• Enlarging a major interval by a half step turns it into an **augmented** interval: C–A♯ is an augmented sixth.

minor ⟵ *reduce* — **major** — *enlarge* ⟶ **augmented**

Minor reduced once more
A minor interval can be made smaller once more; it then becomes a *diminished interval*.

FIFTEEN INTERVALS

The fifteen most common intervals are shown on the next page. The perfect and major intervals are listed below the keyboard; the minor and diminished intervals are printed above the keyboard, and the augmented intervals are on the first line. Other intervals, such as the augmented unison (C–C♯), are quite rare.

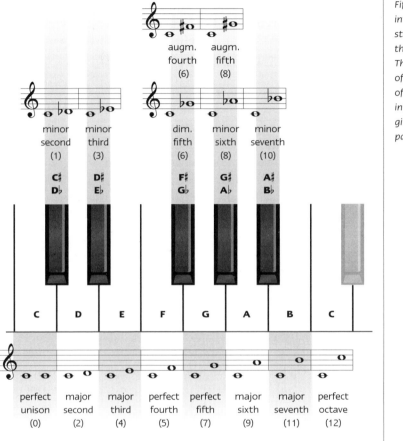

Fifteen
intervals
starting on
the root C.
The number
of half steps
of each
interval is
given in
parentheses.

dim. = *diminished* augm. = *augmented*

Same sound, different name

Just as there are enharmonic notes (see page 48), there are
enharmonic intervals too. They are intervals that use the same
piano keys or the same fingerings, but they have different names.
For example, C–G♯ is an augmented fifth and C–A♭ is a minor
sixth, but both intervals span the same number of half steps, and
you play them using the same keys.

Larger intervals

All the intervals introduced so far have been within the space
of one octave. To name larger intervals, you just keep counting.
From C to the D of the next octave is a major *ninth*; from C to E

111

in the next octave is a major *tenth*, and so on. These are *compound intervals*: intervals that are made up of an octave plus a second interval. You'll be seeing a lot of these intervals when you use chord symbols (see page 154 and pages 218–221).

Major up, minor down

If you go from C to a higher sounding E, it's a major third. If you go from C to the E below, you're playing a minor sixth. The same goes for every other pair of notes that form a major interval one way: They form a minor interval when inverted — i.e., when the lower note and the higher one switch positions. Major scales consist of perfect and major intervals when you go upward from the root. But going down (C to the B below, C to the A below, and so on) you'll find perfect and minor intervals only.

Tipcode MOP-038

The scale

A potential mistake: On a piano keyboard, F–B may look like a perfect fourth, as it spans four white notes, just like C–F. But F–B is not a perfect fourth; it's an augmented fourth. If you want to name an interval, you need to take the major scale of the root note into account. In F major, the fourth step is B♭, so F–B♭ is a perfect fourth; F–B is an augmented fourth.

TIP

Complementary intervals

Two intervals that make up an octave (e.g., C to the E above, plus C to the E below), are known as complementary intervals. They have the same letters, but different directions. As shown in the Major up, minor down paragraph, the complement of a minor interval is always a major interval, and perfect intervals are complemented by perfect intervals. If you go up a major third (C–E, ascending), the complement is a minor sixth (C–E, descending). Note that this equation add up to nine, and so do all other complementary intervals!

Half steps

If you're not sure, you can always count the number of half steps the interval takes. A perfect fifth, for example, spans seven half steps. If it takes eight half steps to get from the first to the second note of the interval, you're looking at an augmented fifth or a minor sixth. The number of half steps for each interval are given in parentheses in the diagram on page 111.

Tritone

The enharmonic augmented fourth (C–F♯) and diminished fifth (C–G♭) are also known as a *tritone*: an interval spanning three whole steps (C-D, D-E, E-F♯ or E-G♭). From this note to the C above, is another tritone.

Tipcode MOP-039

Harmonic and melodic intervals

If you play the two notes of an interval simultaneously, you will hear a harmonic interval. A harmony consists of notes that sound together. If you play the two notes consecutively, you'll hear a melodic interval: A melody is made up of a series of consecutive notes.

CONSONANT AND DISSONANT

Intervals can also be classified as either dissonant or consonant.

Dissonant

Dissonant literally means 'not sounding (well) together'. The notes in a *dissonant interval* seem to disagree, or to create some kind of tension.

The name's obvious

The dissonant intervals are the minor and major seconds, the

113

enharmonic augmented fourth and diminished fifth, and the minor and major sevenths. There's no need to learn these intervals by heart. Just play them, and you'll hear why they're called dissonant.

> **Tipcode MOP-040**

Consonant

Consonant is the opposite of dissonant; the word means 'sounding (well) together'. The notes in a *consonant interval* seem to blend into each other. They offer the release that the tension in dissonant intervals seems to ask for.

(Im)perfect consonant

The consonant intervals can be subdivided once more into *perfect* and *imperfect consonant* intervals. The imperfect ones just sound a bit less 'perfect' or pure. Again, listening to these intervals clearly demonstrates their names.

> **Tipcode MOP-041**

- **Perfect consonant** intervals are the perfect unison, fourth, fifth, and the octave.

- **Imperfect consonant** intervals are the major and minor thirds, and the major and minor sixths.

Release

Composers love to use the flux and play between the tension of dissonant intervals and the release offered by the consonant ones. If you play the notes C–F♯ simultaneously, followed by C–G, you'll hear what's happening: tension and release.

> **Tipcode MOP-042**

114

Good to know

- The octave (and the unison) is the 'most consonant' interval. If you play two Cs or two G's simultaneously on a piano, you can hardly tell that you're listening to two notes: **They sound like one**.

- Dissonant intervals may sound **out of tune** — but they're not. An interval can only be out of tune if the instrument you're playing hasn't been tuned, or if your intonation is off.

- Complementary intervals (see page 112) are always either **consonant or dissonant**. After all, the combination of a C with a lower E is bound to have the same characteristics as a C with a higher E.

INTERVAL RECOGNITION

It is definitely useful to learn to recognize intervals by ear, and to be able to sing them or imagine their sound as you see them in your charts. The latter will allow you to sing a melody or even chords as you are reading the music, while the ability to recognize intervals as your hear them makes it a lot easier to write music or to transcribe songs.

Ear training
One way to learn how to recognize intervals is by figuring out melodies on your instrument, without using sheet music. You can also have someone play intervals for you, while you try to recognize them. Alternatively, there are computer programs, websites, and other media that offer this kind of _ear training_. (Search 'ear training exercises' online, for example.)

Well-known tunes
The easiest way to remember the sound of an interval is simply to

115

sing a tune that begins with that interval. Here are some examples. If you don't know one or more of these songs, go to YouTube or a similar website to hear them online.

Major first	*One Note Samba*
Minor second	*Symphony no. 40 (W.A. Mozart)*
Major second	*Frère Jacques, Frère Jacques*
Minor third	*Greensleeves: 'Alas, my love'*
Major third	*Oh, When the Saints*
Perfect fourth	*Amazing Grace*
Augmented fourth	*Maria (West Side Story)*
Perfect fifth	*Twinkle Twinkle Little Star; It Ain't Necessarily So*
Major sixth	*My Bonnie Lies Over the Ocean*
Minor seventh	*Somewhere: 'There's a place for us'*
Octave	*Somewhere Over the Rainbow*

TIP

Relative pitch and perfect pitch

If you hear two notes and you can tell the interval, you have relative pitch: You can tell the relationship between those notes by ear. If you can tell the pitch of a note as soon as you hear it, or if you can sing a perfect A or any other note without any reference pitch, you have absolute pitch or perfect pitch. People with perfect pitch can typically tell you the name of a chord as they hear it, listing all its notes if desired. Improving your relative pitch is a matter of training. Perfect pitch takes a lot more.

13

More About Major and Minor

There's more to major and minor than what you've read up to now. The following chapter covers variations on the minor scale, relative keys, and how to figure out the key signature of a piece. Apart from enhancing your understanding of music, this information will be useful if you would like to transcribe songs or to compose.

Most Western music is written either in a major or a minor key. They are the two most important modes or scales. Both modes can be indicated in several ways.

Major

If a piece is just said to be 'in G,' it is in G major. To prevent confusion, however, the word major or its abbreviation maj. may be written after the initial letter that indicates the root of the scale. In classical music you may also come across the German word for major, *dur*.

Minor

A minor key or chord is usually specified by the word minor, or the abbreviations min or m after the letter: Cm is C minor. Other ways to indicate the minor mode are a minus sign (C–), a lower-case letter (c) or the German word for minor, *moll*.

Major	Minor
upper case (C)	lower case (c)
maj.	min, m, –
dur (German)	moll (German)

THE LEADING NOTE

If you're listening to a composition in a major scale, you will often hear that the second last note leads to the final note of the melody. This is a result of the half step between the seventh note and the eight note (the second root or tonic) of the scale. This seventh note is known as a *leading note*.

Leading note

In C major, this leading note is the B. In the following example you can clearly hear how B leads to C, half a step upward.

Leading tone and subtonic

The leading note or leading tone is also known as the *subtonic*

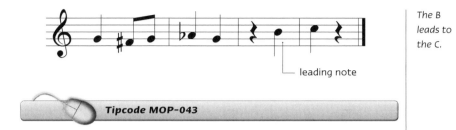

leading note

The B
leads to
the C.

Tipcode MOP-043

— the note that is literally right 'under the tonic', in this case the second root note of the scale.

Not always

The leading note is very important in classical music, but it's not in many other styles of music. For example, there are thousands of rock songs in a major key that actually have a flatted seventh. This turns the last half step of the scale into a whole step. As a result, there is no leading note: Contrary to B, the note B♭ does not lead to C. Note that this major scale is also known as the *Mixolydian mode* (e.g., C D E F G A B♭ C; see page 129).

Minor: (no) leading note

The original minor mode has a whole step between the seventh and eighth notes as well, so the seventh note is not a leading note. However, there are two variations on the minor mode that do have a leading note: melodic minor and harmonic minor.

MELODIC AND HARMONIC MINOR

The first tune on the following page, in D minor, lacks a leading note. In the second tune, the seventh step of D minor (C) is raised to C♯. This turns it into a leading note. If you play this tune, you'll hear how this note clearly leads the melody toward the final D.

Up or down

So altering a minor scale by raising the seventh note provides you

119

D-minor
without
a leading
note.

The same
tune, now
with a
leading
note.

Tipcode MOP-044

with a leading note. This altered minor mode is known as *melodic minor*. Because the leading note always wants to rise to the root, it is used for ascending melodies only. When descending, melodic minor is identical to pure or natural minor.

Raise the sixth step too

In the ascending version of melodic minor, the sixth step is raised too. Why? Raising the seventh step to form a leading note creates a gap of three half steps between the sixth and seventh steps. (In C, this would be from A♭ to the raised B.) Raising the sixth reduces the gap to a whole step (A–B).

Tipcode MOP-045

One difference

With that, the only difference between a major scale and the ascending melodic minor scale with the same root is the lowered

Tetrachords

Both minor and major scales can be split in two halves. Each half is a tetrachord. A major scale is made up of two tetra-chords with identical whole and half steps (e.g., C D E F and G A B C). In melodic minor, the first tetrachord is minor (C D E♭ F), the second is major (G A B C).

120

third. After all, the lowered sixth and seventh steps have been raised to their original pitches: C melodic minor is C D E♭ F G A B C.

Harmonic minor

Harmonic minor is another alteration of the minor scale. It has a raised seventh; the third and sixth remain lowered. As a result, this scale has the large gap between the sixth (A♭) and seventh (B) step (e.g., C D E♭ F G A♭ B C).

Accidentals

The ascending melodic minor scale and the harmonic minor scale are alterations of the natural minor scale. This means that you won't find a piece 'in G harmonic minor,' for example: Melodic and harmonic minor are scored with accidentals. The example below is in D minor, which has one flat in the key signature. The two accidentals come from the ascending melodic minor scale.

Tune in D minor using the ascending melodic minor scale; the B♭ is raised with a natural sign.

RELATIVE MAJOR AND MINOR

If you want to transcribe a song from a CD, for example, you need to know which key it is in. In order to do so, you need to know a bit more about scales.

Two scales

All major and minor scales have been listed in Chapter 10. If you look at the tables on pages 94 and 97, you'll see that there are two scales without flats and sharps (C major on the first line of the table on page 94; A minor on the first line of the table on page 97). There are also two scales with one sharp, two scales with three sharps, two scales with four, and so on.

Relative scales
These pairs of scales, using the same notes and the same key signature, are *relative scales* or *relative keys*. For example, A minor (A B C D E F G A) is the *relative minor* of C major (C D E F G A B C): The actual notes of these scales, though in a different order, are the same. The key signature is the same as well, but the scales have a different root.

Two sharps, two flats
Likewise, D major (two sharps) is the *relative major* of B minor (again, two sharps); G minor (two flats) is the relative minor of B♭ major (again, two flats).

Relative minor
Finding the relative minor of a given major scale is simply a matter of counting. The relative minor is always indicated by the sixth step of the major scale. Two examples:

• D minor is the **relative minor** of F major; D is the sixth step of F major (F G A B♭ C **D** E F).

• E minor is the **relative minor** of G major; E is the sixth step of G major (G A B C D **E** F♯ G).

Relative major
You will find the relative major of a minor key by looking at the third step of the minor scale. Two examples:

• C major is the **relative major** of A minor (A B **C** D E F G A).

• The **relative major** of C minor (C D **E♭** F G A♭ B♭ C) is E♭ major.

Once again: the circle of fifths
When fitting the minor keys into the circle of fifths, they are automatically paired with their relative major keys: Minor keys and their relative major keys have the same clock position (e.g., C and A minor at 12 o'clock, G and E minor at 1 o'clock, etc.)

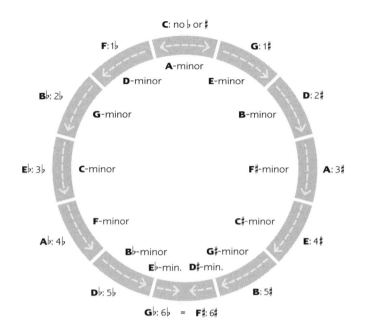

The circle of
fifths showing
the relative
major keys
(outer circle)
and minor keys
(inner circle).

Parallel keys

Relative keys may be confused with *parallel keys*. The difference?
Relative keys have the same key signature and a different root.
Parallel keys have the same root and a different key signature, such
as C major (no sharps, no flats) and C minor (three flats).

FIGURING OUT KEYS

It's often useful to be able to figure out what key a piece is in,
whether you're playing from sheet music, transcribing a song from
a recording, or playing a solo over prerecorded music.

First: the root

To figure out the key of a piece of music, you first need to find its
root note. This is nearly always the note a melody ends on. The
moment you feel the song is over, you're typically listening to the
root. In the following two melodies it is fairly easy to sense what

123

the root is. If you play them and stop right before the last note, you will probably be able to sing it before you play it: It's the root or the home note. If you don't have an instrument at hand, listen to Tipcode MOP-046 instead.

If you play these melodies, you can 'hear' the last note before you've played it.

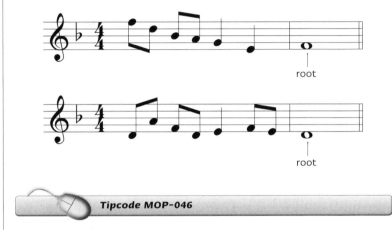

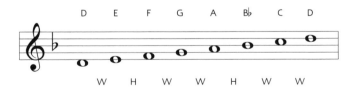

F major or D minor?

Both melodies above have a single flat in the key signature. The circle of fifths on the previous page indicates that a single flat tells you that these melodies are either in F major or its relative D minor. Which one is it? The root note at the end usually provides the correct answer. The first tune ends on an F, so it's in F major; the second one ends on D, and it's in D minor.

The D-minor scale.

Trick

If you're looking at a key signature and you don't remember which minor or major keys the flats or sharps in the key signature refer to (and you don't have a circle of fifths at hand to tell you), here's what you can do.

Pointing sharps

If it's a key signature with sharps, then look at the final sharp, and go a half step up. This note is the root note if the piece is in a major key. If not, it's in its relative minor key.

The last sharp (D♯) points to the E. Therefore the key is E-major, or its relative, C♯-minor.

The second-to-last flat

In flat key signatures, it's even easier. The second-to-last flat tells you the possible major key. If it's in minor, it's the relative minor of that key.

The second-to-last flat refers to the A♭, so this piece is in A♭-major, or its relative, F-minor.

BY EAR

Figuring out the key of a piece of music by ear, from a CD for example, is a bit harder.

• First figure out **the root** by listening to the final note of the piece, or by listening to other sections where the melody seems to come to a rest.

• Sing the root when you have found it, and use an instrument to find out **which note** it is.

• Now try out both the major and minor scales that begin with that note (they're all written out on pages 211 and 212). In most cases, you'll be able to hear which of the two scales best matches the music. This will usually be **the key**.

Sounds easier

The above sounds easier than it really is, especially if you're just

125

starting out. A tip: First try this with very basic, familiar melodies such as children's songs.

14

Other Scales

Major and minor scales are each made up of five whole and two half steps in specific orders. By changing the order of those steps, you can create another five scales. In addition, there are scales that use different intervals altogether: half steps or whole steps only, for example. This chapter takes you from medieval church music to modal jazz, and from China to the blues.

In Chapter 10, the C major and A minor scales were illustrated using a circle made up of half steps and whole steps, using C and A as starting points respectively.

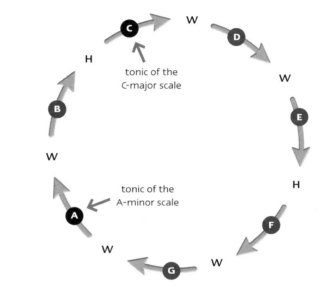

Different orders
If you use any of the other notes as a starting point, you will hear five more scales, each with its own character.

Traditional modes
The resulting seven scales (one for each white note) are usually referred to as the *traditional modes* or *church modes*: They go back to the Roman Catholic church music in the Middle Ages.

White notes
Each of these scales can of course be played using white notes only, as shown on the opposite page.

Major and minor
As you can see, the *Ionian mode* is identical to the modern major scale; the *Aeolian mode* is similar to the natural minor scale. These two scales were added in the sixteenth century.

Mode	A.k.a.	Played on white notes	Whole and half steps						
Ionian	C-mode	C D E F G A B C	W	W	H	W	W	W	H
Dorian	D-mode	D E F G A B C D	W	H	W	W	W	H	W
Phrygian	E-mode	E F G A B C D E	H	W	W	W	H	W	W
Lydian	F-mode	F G A B C D E F	W	W	W	H	W	W	H
Mixolydian	G-mode	G A B C D E F G	W	W	H	W	W	H	W
Aeolian	A-mode	A B C D E F G A	W	H	W	W	H	W	W
Locrian	B-mode	B C D E F G A B	H	W	W	H	W	W	W

Diatonic scales

These seven modes are also known as the *diatonic scales*. All diatonic scales are made up of five whole and two half steps in a specific order.

TIP

> ## Mnemonics
>
> *There are many memory joggers to help you remember the order of the traditional modes (Ionian, Dorian, etc.), including:*
>
> - **If Dora Plays Like Me, All's Lost**
> - **I Don't Particularly Like Modes A Lot**
> - **I Don't Play Loud Music After Lunch**
> - **I Don't Play Like My Aunt Lucy**

Different characters

If you play around with these modes or scales a bit, rather than just playing them up and down the scale, you will get to hear their specific characters. Some examples? The *Mixolydian mode* is often heard in pop songs and boogie-woogie. Playing around in the *Phrygian mode* may make you think of Spanish music, and the *Locrian mode* tends to sound jazzy.

Listen

To hear the differences from one scale to another, it's best to play

129

them all from C. This requires you to copy the orders of their whole and half steps for each scale, of course. As an example, here are the *Lydian* and *Locrian* scales or modes, both starting on C.

C Lydian

C Locrian

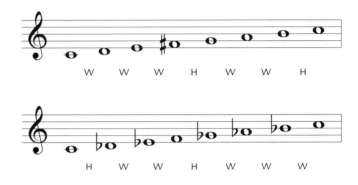

Modal music

The term *modal music* is sometimes used to indicate music in which the character of a traditional mode is clearly identifiable. Usually there's not much harmonic activity in this type of music, and you won't hear too many chord changes. In classical music, the church modes weren't used much from around 1600 until the late nineteenth century, when certain composers started using them again.

Modal jazz

There's also non-classical modal music. In the late 1950s jazz trumpeter Miles Davis stopped relying on the chord changes that were essential in bebop, the style of jazz that was developed in the 1940s. Davis then started what became known as modal jazz. His album 'Kind of Blue' (1959) clearly demonstrates what that sounds like. Listen to Davis' music on YouTube, Spotify, or other websites.

NON-DIATONIC SCALES

The scales in the following section use different combinations of whole and half steps: These are non-diatonic scales.

Chromatic

The *chromatic scale* uses all twelve notes in the octave: It has half steps only. This scale is great for practicing, just going up and down, playing every single note on your instrument. A variation: Start on another note each time. You'll find this scale — and many ways to fool around with it — in lots of exercise books.

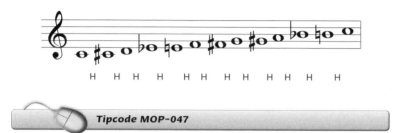

The chromatic scale.

H H H   H   H H   H H   H H   H   H

Tipcode MOP-047

Hexatonic

The *hexatonic scale* or *whole-tone scale* consists of whole steps only, which results in a six-note scale (not counting high C, i.e., the second root note). Hexa means six.

Hexatonic scale.

W   W   W   W   W   W

TIP

Two

There are two hexatonic scales only: One that includes the note C (C D E F♯ G♯ A♯), and one that includes the note C♯ (C♯ D♯ F G A B).

Octatonic

Octatonic scales are eight-note scales (octa means eight, as in octave) with alternating half and whole steps. They are mainly used in jazz and twentieth-century classical music. There are two versions: one starting with a whole step, the other starting with a half step. The latter is pictured on the following page.

*An octatonic
scale, starting
with a half
step.*

H   W   H   W   H   W   H   W

Pentatonic scales
Pentatonic scales have five different notes (penta = five). They're
used in many different styles: You can hear them in country, pop,
and folk, but they can have a definite Chinese flavor as well. Want
to hear that flavor? Try playing two-note combinations of black
keys, keeping one black key between each pair (e.g., F♯–A♯, G♯–C♯,
A♯–D♯).

*A pentatonic
scale.*

W   W   HHH   W   HHH

Minor pentatonic
There is a *minor pentatonic scale* as well: C E♭ F G B♭.

Blues scales
There are several *blues scales.* Pictured below is a classic one.
Basically, it is the same scale as the minor pentatonic scale, yet
with an added F♯. Others indicate this note as a G♭.

*A classic
blues scale.*

HHH   W   H   H   HHH   W

The gypsy scale
The so-called *gypsy scale* has a clearly identifiable sound. Just like
the blues scale, it has two intervals of three half steps (E♭–F♯ and
A♭–B).

The gypsy scale.

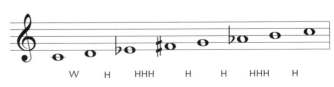

W   H   HHH   H   H   HHH   H

15

Transposition

Many wind instruments — trumpets, saxophones, and so on — sound a different note than the one shown on paper. They are known as transposing instruments. If you want to write music for transposing instruments, you need to transpose it the music, i.e., convert the music to another scale. Knowing how to do this also allows you to change the key of a song if it needs to be played one or more steps higher or lower.

When tenor sax players see a C5 on paper (see pages 135 and 215), they close the key under their left middle finger: They finger a C. When they blow, though, the note you hear is a B♭, a whole step lower.

B♭ instruments

In other words: On a tenor saxophone, a fingered C results in a *sounding B♭* (*B♭ concert pitch*). Hence, the tenor saxophone is known as a B♭ instrument. Soprano saxophones are in B♭ as well, and so are most trumpets and clarinets.

E♭ instruments

E♭ instruments, such as alto and baritone saxophones, sound an E♭ when the player sees and fingers a C.

Two transposing instruments. The tenor saxophone (left) is a B♭ instrument; the alto sax is in E♭.

The same fingering

This may sound a little complicated, but it has one great advantage. No matter which sax voice you're playing (tenor, alto, etc.), you always use the same fingerings: A C5 on paper always tells you to close the key under your left middle finger. The note you'll hear is the note the composer wanted to hear: The saxophone 'transposes' the written note to the desired pitch. The illustration below shows you what a printed C5 sounds like when played on the four most popular saxophone voices.

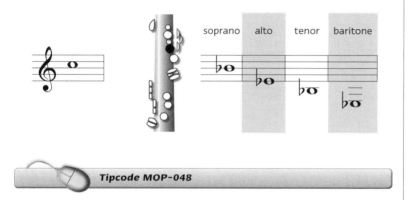

The written note C5, the corresponding fingering, and the concert pitches on four saxophones.

Tipcode MOP-048

Lower sound, higher note

As you can see, the soprano saxophone sounds a whole step lower than the written note: C5 on paper produces a sounding B♭4. In other words: If the composer wants to hear a B♭4, they put a C on paper. The tenor saxophone sounds a ninth lower than the written note: C5 produces B♭3, so composers write every note for this instrument a ninth higher than the concert pitch they want to hear.

Other instruments and tunings

There are many transposing wind instruments. Some examples of popular instruments:

- Most **trumpets** are in B♭, but there are trumpets in C, D, F, and other tunings too.

- Most **other brass instruments** are transposing instruments as well, such as the tuba, available in various sizes and in C, B♭, F, and other tunings, and the French horn (in B♭ and F).

- The most popular **clarinet** is the B♭ clarinet. Symphonic players often use an A clarinet as well, and there is a smaller clarinet and an alto clarinet in E♭, among other clarinet voices.

- The standard concert flute is in C, but the larger **alto flute** is in G.

An octave

For some instruments, the music is written either an octave higher or lower than it sounds. Music for guitar and bass, for example, is written an octave higher than these instruments sound, while music for the high-pitched piccolo is written an octave lower. This practice saves using lots of ledger lines: The lowest note of a regular bass guitar or double bass would otherwise require four of these lines (see page 215). Because a fingered C still produces a C on all of these instruments, they're not classified as transposing instruments.

TIP

Why not in C

You may wonder why most instruments are in different keys, or why most trumpeters play a B♭ trumpet while C trumpets are available too. The answer is quite simple. To make a trumpet sound in C (a whole step higher than B♭), it needs to be smaller than the lower sounding B♭ trumpet. The smaller size not only makes it sound higher, but it makes for a slightly different timbre as well: the tone gets a bit brighter, for example — and most trumpeters and composers simply seem to prefer the slightly darker or bigger tone of the slightly larger B♭ trumpet. Likewise, clarinet players and most composers typically opt for the standard B♭ clarinet. The A clarinet, only a half step lower, sounds markedly darker, sweeter, or warmer, which is the preferred sound for various compositions.

TRANSPOSING

If you write music for transposing instruments, you have to be able to transpose. You also have to transpose if you want to play a piece in another key, for example because the vocalist in the band can't manage to sing the highest notes in a song. Transposing the song to a lower key solves the problem. Also, transposing a song can make certain guitar chords easier to finger.

Sounds harder than it is

Transposing sounds harder than it is. Without knowing it, you've already transposed 'Twinkle, Twinkle' from C to F and also to D in Chapter 4. Transposing music also demonstrates how efficient the system of sharps and flats actually is.

Automatic transposition

If you use a music notation program (see page 180), transposing music is usually a matter of a few mouse clicks — but even then it's good to know how it works.

TIP

In a nutshell

Basically, transposing is a matter of changing the key signature to the new key and moving all the notes to their new positions on the staff.

Here's how

Say you want to transpose a melody from C major to E♭ major. This makes it sound a minor third higher (from C to E♭ is a minor third).

* E♭ major has **three flats**, as the circle of fifths tells you (see page 123).

* **Jot down** these flats (B♭, E♭, A♭) next to the clef, in their proper positions (see page 46).

* E♭ is a minor third higher than C. A third implies that you have

137

to move all the notes **three positions up**, including the position of the original note (C=1, D=2, E=3).

- The three flats **automatically** turn all Bs into B♭s, all As into A♭s, and all Es into E♭s.

- **You're done!**

'Twinkle,
Twinkle'
transposed from
C to E♭. The
three flats are
at the clef. The
original notes
are in gray; the
new notes in
black.

Twin – kle twin – kle   lit – tle   star

Naturals, sharps, and flats
So really, transposing is no more than figuring out the sharps and flats of the new key, and moving the notes up or down on the staff. The required sharps or flats can be found in the circle of fifths or on pages 94 and 97. The name of the interval tells you how far you have to move the notes up or down: two positions if it's a second, three if it's a third, and so on.

A major third
Transposing from C to E♭, 'Twinkle, Twinkle' went up a minor third. If you want to transpose the same tune from C to E (now a major third), the notes will be moved to the same positions as in the above example, but the key signature will have four sharps: E major has four sharps, which will automatically raise the four corresponding notes.

From E♭ to B
Transposing a piece from E♭ to B is just as easy as from C to E♭, for example:

- B major has **five sharps**. Write them down next to the clef.

- The interval E♭–B is an **augmented fifth** (E♭, F, G, A, B).

- A fifth implies that the notes have to be moved upward **five positions**, again including the original and final positions. Every first line E♭ will be a third line B (E♭=1, F=2, G=3, A=4, B=5), and so on.

Twin – kle   Twin – kle   lit – tle   star

'Twinkle, Twinkle'
transposed from
Eb to B. The
original notes are
in gray, the new
notes in black.
The three flats
of Eb-major have
been replaced by
the five sharps of
B-major.

Transposing accidentals

If one or more notes have accidentals, things get a little bit more complicated: A sharp or flat sign may need to be turned into a natural sign, or vice versa. In the following example, a melody is transposed from Bb major to G major. The new key signature is put in place (one sharp), and the notes are moved three places down the staff.

A tune
transposed
from Bb-major
to G-major. The
natural sign
becomes
a sharp.

Example

In the original melody, a natural sign raised the fourth step of Bb major (Eb) to an E. Therefore, the fourth step in G major (C) has to be raised too, so the C gets a sharp, turning it into a C#.

16

Time, Meter, and Rhythm

A chapter on strong beats and weak beats, syncopation,
odd time signatures, single and compound meters,
swing, and the clave.

In a piece in $\frac{4}{4}$ you can usually hear pretty easily where the first beat is: This beat sounds or feels a little stronger than the rest, which is why it's known as the *strong beat* or *natural accent*. The third beat, though slightly less strong, is also referred to as a natural accent. Two and four are the weak beats in $\frac{4}{4}$.

Downbeat
Other names for the first and third beats are *accented beats*, *principal metric accents*, or *downbeats*. The last term turns beats two and four into *upbeats* (or *offbeats*, sometimes).

Pop, rock, jazz
In most pop and rock tunes, the snare drum clearly accents the 'weak' second and fourth beats, which are then known as the *after-beats* or *backbeats*. No matter how loudly the drummer is banging out 2 and 4, the first and third beats still tend to feel stronger.

Syncopation
Composers and musicians can place accents on the weak beats of the bar or on notes that would normally not be stressed, or vice versa. Notes may also be played earlier or later than expected. This is known as syncopation. Here's an example. Syncopation is often used in styles such as jazz, rap, salsa, fusion, progressive rock, and Afrocuban music.

The four last notes of the first bar are syncopated notes.

Tipcode MOP-062

Meter
The time signature of a piece specifies both the number of beats per bar and the counting unit, e.g., half notes, quarter notes, or eighth notes. The meter tells you the way in which the beats of a piece are arranged into measures or bars. Quadruple meter has four beats per bar (e.g., $\frac{4}{4}$), triple meter or triple time has three (e.g., $\frac{3}{8}$), and duple meter two beats per bar.

Simple and common

Duple, triple, and quadruple meter are *common meters* or *simple meters*.

Compound meters

Meters with a triple pulse per beat are known as *compound meters*. For example, $\frac{6}{8}$ is compound duple meter; each bar consisting of two (duple) groups of three; $\frac{9}{8}$ is compound triple meter.

Two groups of three: $\frac{6}{4}$ and $\frac{6}{8}$

In pieces in $\frac{6}{4}$ and $\frac{6}{8}$, each bar is usually felt as two groups of three notes. That's why $\frac{6}{8}$ is often counted in two (1-and-ah 2-and-ah) rather than as 1, 2, 3, 4, 5, 6. Each of these two 'beats' equals a dotted quarter note, which can be divided into three (eighth notes) — a characteristic of compound time.

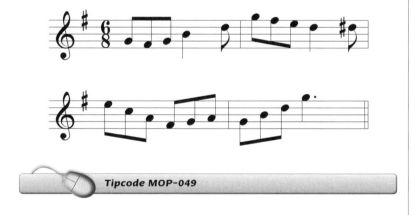

Two groups of three in every bar: a melody in $\frac{6}{8}$.

Tipcode MOP-049

ODD TIME SIGNATURES

In *irregular* or *odd time signatures* each bar consists of one or more groups of two and three beats, such as $\frac{5}{4}$ (2+3) or $\frac{10}{8}$ (2+2+3+3). Odd time signatures are quite uncommon in Western music. Note that the exact order of these groups may vary from composition to composition!

143

Counting in groups

When counting along in an odd time signature, you will typically follow these smaller groupings. For example, $\frac{5}{4}$ will be counted as 1, 2, 3, 1, 2, or the other way around, as 1, 2, 1, 2, 3. Which one you choose depends on the division of strong and weak beats in the piece. You can also count the groups themselves rather than the individual beats, e.g. 1-and 2-and-ah or 1-and-ah 2-and.

Tipcode MOP-050

Take Five

One of the few really well-known pieces in $\frac{5}{4}$ is the jazz standard 'Take Five,' written in the late 1950s. In this piece, the strong beats are on 1 and 4, dividing each bar up into groups of three and two (1, 2, 3; 1, 2), just like the following example.

Tune in $\frac{5}{4}$.

No doubt

You can usually hear whether a piece in $\frac{5}{4}$ needs to be counted as a group of two followed by a group of three, or vice versa. Still, you may come across the following time signature, leaving nothing to doubt.

A $\frac{5}{4}$ time signature divided into 3+2.

Dotted bar lines

Likewise, you may find a $^{3+2+4}$ time signature, for example. To make such bars easier to read, dotted or dashed bar lines can be used in between the regular bar lines, separating the three smaller groups of beats.

Changing time signatures

In some compositions, the time signature changes one or more times throughout the piece. As an example, you may want to check out the famous work *Le sacre du printemps* (*The Rite of Spring*) by Igor Strawinsky, who changed the time signature per bar at some points.

> ## Kind gesture
>
> *If a new time signature is introduced at the beginning of a next line, you may not see it in time. That's why some composers print this time signature at the end of the preceding line as well, warning you in time. This is known as a courtesy time signature or cautionary time signature. Printed music may also contain courtesy clefs and courtesy key signatures, telling you that you are about to switch to another clef or key.*

TIP

SWING

The word swing is used mostly in jazz. In swing style, eighth notes are played and felt more as triplets than as regular, 'straight' eighth notes: The music has a *triplet feel*.

In eighths

To indicate that a piece needs to be played with a triplet feel or swing feel, rather than the written eight notes, the word 'swing' is printed above the first line. Alternatively, you'll see the two eight notes equaling a (quarter note/eighth note) triplet, as shown here.

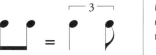

Play the eighth notes with a triplet feel.

145

Tipcode MOP-051

Drummers

Jazz drummers use a slightly different notation of that same rhythm, shown in the ride cymbal pattern that is printed above the fifth line. When playing this basic jazz beat, the hi-hat cymbals are usually closed on beats 2 and 4, as indicated by the cross-shaped notes below the first line.

Basic jazz beat (swing).

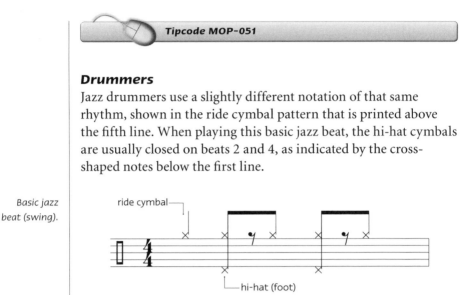

ride cymbal

hi-hat (foot)

Up tempo

At high tempos, the ride beat sounds more like a pattern with eighth notes, as shown below.

At high tempos.

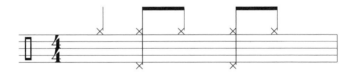

Ballads

At really slow tempos, the second note of the second and fourth beat moves the other way, closer to the third and first beats. As a result, it will sound more or less like this — without playing true sixteenth notes:

At low tempos.

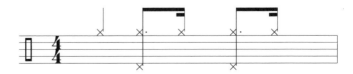

Straight eighths

Some pieces have sections that you play as swing, and others where you have to play straight eighth notes. The latter sections are then indicated with the terms *straight eighths, even eighths,* or *even 8ths.*

THE CLAVE

Most classical compositions, and pop, rock, or jazz pieces have one or two accented beats per bar. Latin American music, on the contrary, is typically based on the clave, a five-note pattern that is played over two bars. Popular claves include the son clave, the rumba clave, and the § clave. The examples below start with two notes in the first bar, and three in the second. This pattern may be inverted as well, turning it into a 3-2 son clave rather than the pictured 2-3 clave. The rumba clave has the third note on the second half of the fourth beat, rather than on four.

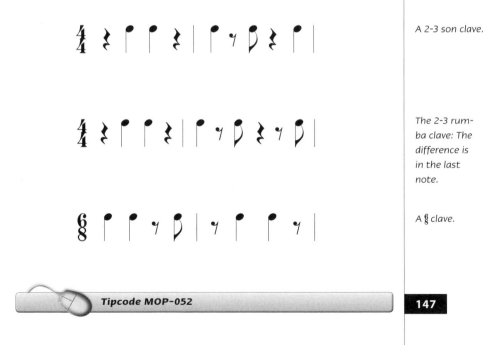

A 2-3 son clave.

The 2-3 rumba clave: The difference is in the last note.

A § clave.

Tipcode MOP-052

POLYRHYTHM

Polyrhythm is the use of different, contrasting rhythms simultaneously. The use of polyrhythm is common in jazz and traditional African music, for example. A basic and popular example is playing three against two: You do so when you play quarter-note triplets (see pages 33–34) against quarter notes, as shown below. Likewise, you can play duplets in ⅜ or ⁶⁄₄, for example.

Three against two.

17

Do, Re, Mi - I, II, III

In Chapter 2, the octave was illustrated using the sequence Do Re Mi Fa Sol La Ti Do. These syllables are another way of indicating notes. Instead, Arabic and Roman numbers can be used as well.

The sequence Do, Re, Mi (etc.) is used in two ways: either with a *permanent Do* or *fixed Do*, where Do always represents C, or with a *movable Do.*

Major scale
The movable Do represents the first note of any major scale: Do is the root or tonic of that scale. If you sing Do, Re, Mi (etc.) starting on an A, you'll be singing the scale of A major. If you start on a C♯ you'll be singing the scale of C♯ major instead — and so on.

The fixed Do
In some countries, such as France and Spain, Do always represents C (so it's a fixed Do). In France, C major is referred to as Do major, and E major is Mi major, for example.

Solmization
This system of assigning syllables to the white notes is known as *solmization.* It's also referred to as *solfege.*

TIP

> ## Singing a minor scale
> *If you sing Do, Re, Mi starting on Do, you'll be singing a major scale. Starting on La will result in a minor scale, if you do it correctly. Use a keyboard or a piano to check if you do, because you may still sing a major scale!*

Black notes
The solmization system includes names for the half steps too.

• When a note is **raised**, the vowel in the syllable changes to an i (pronounced as an 'e'), just like the syllables at the two half steps in the major scale (Mi and Ti). Here's the chromatic scale with raised notes: Do, Di, Re, Ri, Mi, Fa, Fi, Sol, Si, La, Li, Ti, Do.

• If the note is **lowered**, the vowel becomes an a (say 'ah') or an e: Do, Ra, Re, Me, Mi, Fa, Se, Sol, Le, La, Te, Ti, Do.

Trick
You can use these sequences to figure out the notes of a scale. If

you want to find out the scale of A major, jot down the chromatic scale of A under the Do-Re-Mi scale, and see which notes line up with those 'white' syllables, and so on. The result is the scale of A major: A, B, C♯ D, etc.

Do	Do♯	Re	Re♯	Mi	Fa	Fa♯	Sol	Sol♯	La	La♯	Ti	Do
C	C♯	D	D♯	E	F	F♯	G	G♯	A	A♯	B	C

Flats

You can use the same trick for scales that have one or more flats in the key signature, such as F major. The 'white' syllables automatically correspond with the notes of that major scale: F, G, A, B♭, and so on.

Do	Re♭	Re	Mi♭	Mi	Fa	Sol♭	Sol	La♭	La	Ti♭	Ti	Do
C	D♭	D	E♭	E	F	G♭	G	A♭	A	B♭	B	C

1,2,3 – I, II, III

Instead of using these syllables, you can indicate the steps of a scale with numbers, sharps and flats. This allows you to easily figure out the notes of a specific scale. The tonic of the scale (Do) is 1, the second note is 2, and so on.

Minor scale

A regular minor scale, (with its lowered third, sixth and seventh steps) would then look as 1 2 ♭3 4 5 ♭6 ♭7 8.

1	2	♭3	4	5	♭6	♭7	8
C	D	E♭	F	G	A♭	B♭	C

Chords

Likewise, these numbers can be used to indicate the notes of chords, as shown on 157–159.

151

Roman numerals

Instead of Arabic numbers (1, 2, 3), Roman numerals can be used. Here's the gypsy scale, printed on page 132, again with an example in C printed below the numerals.

I	II	♭III	IV♯	V	♭VI	VII	VIII
C	D	E♭	F♯	G	A♭	B♭	C

Flats and sharps

When using Roman numerals for the white notes of a scale, flats are usually written before the numeral they refer to (e.g., ♭V), while sharps are printed after the number.

Do	Di	Re	Ri	Mi	Fa	Fi	Sol	Si	La	Li	Ti	Do
I	I♯	II	II♯	III	IV	IV♯	V	V♯	VI	VI♯	VII	VIII

Do	Ra	Re	Me	Mi	Fa	Se	Sol	Le	La	Te	Ti	Do
I	♭I	II	♭II	III	IV	♭IV	V	♭V	VI	♭VI	VII	VIII

Roman numerals for chords

The use of Roman numerals to designate the single notes of a scale can be confusing, as many musicians use these numerals to indicate chords and their corresponding degrees of the scale.

18

Chords

Adding chords to a melody makes the music come to life. In songbooks and other printed music sources, chords are often printed as chord symbols, printed above the melody. This chapter tells you what these symbols stand for. It covers chord construction and it tells you about chords functions: what chords do in relationship to each other and the melody. The latter topics belong to the subject of harmony. It can be truly useful to know a bit more about this subject, even if you don't play chords at all (because your instrument doesn't allow for it) or if you're a classical pianist or guitarist, and your sheet music shows your chords note by note rather than as chord symbols.

A chord is typically defined as three or more pitches that sound simultaneously. The chords in a piece are supposed to match, color, and support the melody.

Why?

Why does it make sense to know more about chords? After all, you can simply play the notes printed in your music, or learn all chord symbols and do what they tell you to. Most importantly, understanding chords provides a better understanding of the music you're playing, which in turn can make you a better musician. Knowing more about chords also tends to make it easier to feel where the music is heading, or what the next note or chord will be. This may help you prevent mistakes, or allow you to fix possible mistakes right away. If you play jazz or any other style of music where you're supposed to take solos, you base those solos on the chords of the music, and bass players typically play the bottom notes of the chord of a piece.

Chord symbols

A *chord symbol* tells you which notes to play for a certain chord. It consists of a capital letter that designates the root note of the chord, often followed by one or more numbers and/or abbreviations (see pages 158–159). The music on these two pages shows some examples. There's a comprehensive list of chord symbols on pages 218–221.

Traditional notation

Classical music doesn't use chord symbols. Instead, the notes

'Twinkle, Twinkle' with chords and broken chords.

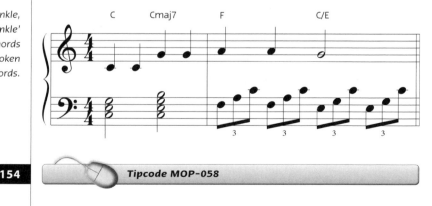

Tipcode MOP-058

Vocal part
with chord
symbols.

Piano part
with chords
in traditional
notation and
chord symbols.

Tipcode MOP-059

that make up the chords are simply printed on the staff, as shown on the previous pages. This traditional notation can be found in many songbooks too.

Broken chords

The notes of the chords can be played simultaneously (see bar 1), or as *broken chords*, playing the notes in succession (see bar 2). The chord symbols in this example are added as an extra.

Twinkle, Twinkle and Mozart

Few people know that the melody of 'Twinkle, Twinkle' is based on the old French folk song, Ah vous dirai je, Maman. Wolfgang Amadeus Mozart (1765–1791) composed twelve variations on this theme, and the same melody was used by other composers and for other children's songs as well, including the famous 'Baa Baa Black Sheep'. If you search the French title on YouTube, you will hear numerous editions of the song, including one or more that Mozart wrote.

CHORDS: THREE PITCHES

Chords always consist of three of more pitches. The intervals between those pitches make for different types of chords, each with their own sound and character.

Types of chords

First of all, there are *major chords* and *minor chords*, with due similarities to major and minor scales, of course. Both of these chord types are made up out of three pitches.

- C major is C–E–G.

- C minor is C–E♭-G.

The difference between the two chords – E♭ replacing E – changes both intervals in the chord, which makes for a major difference in the sound of the chord.

- The major chord consists of the tonic C, a **major** third (C–E) and a **minor** third (E–G).

- The major chord consists of the tonic C, a **minor** third (C–Eb) and a **major** third (Eb–G). Note that the order of the thirds has been inverted.

Stacked thirds

As you can see, both of these chords are constructed of stacked thirds. Such chords are known as *triads*. You can make four, quite different sounding three-note chords, this way:

chord type	notes	thirds	chord name
major	C–E–G	major – minor	C major
minor	C–Eb–G	minor – major	C minor
diminished	C–Eb–Gb	minor – minor	C dim(inished)
augmented	C–E–G♯	major – major	C aug(mented)

Tipcode MOP-060

From the root

Chords with four or more pitches are typically made up of stacked thirds, as you will see later on. Still, it's usually easier to look at the root of the chord and the intervals from that root note to the other notes. The root is usually indicated either with the number 1 or a capital R. The third is a 3, the fifth is a 5, etc.

Major

Following this approach, a major chord is 1–3–5: the root, a major third and a perfect fifth. Sharps and flats can be used to make

chord type	notes	intervals	chord name
major	C–E–G	1 – 3 – 5	C major
minor	C–Eb–G	1 – b3 – 5	C minor
diminished	C–Eb–Gb	1 – b3 – b5	C dim(inished)
augmented	C–E–G♯	1 – 3 – ♯5	C aug(mented)

157

these intervals larger or smaller. With this in mind, have another look at the same three triads, now listing the intervals from the root (see table on the bottom of the previous page).

Chord symbols
As stated before, chords are often shown as chord symbols.

- The first capital represents the root note of the chord. A single capital C is the chord symbol for **C major**.

- A lower case 'm', the abbreviation 'min' or a minus (Cm, Cmin, C-) turn it into the chord symbol for **C minor**.

- C° or Cdim indicates a **diminished** chord.

- Caug is an **augmented** chord.

The list
Most chord symbols are listed on pages 218–221, specifying chord construction, alternative chord symbols, the names of the chords, and examples of each chord in C. Tip: The chord pointers on pages 209–210 allow you to easily play most of these chords on a keyboard instrument!

FOUR AND MORE

The additional pitches in chords of four or more notes are usually designated by numbers. All of these *extensions* can be lowered and raised with flats and sharps.

- The root note followed by **the number 7** indicates a major chord with an added minor seventh: C7 is C–E–G–B♭ (R–3–5–♭7). A *7th chord* consists of four pitches.

- The abbreviation **maj7** or Δ7 turns this four-note chord into a major seventh. Cmaj7 or CΔ7 is C–E–G–B (R–3–5–7). Tip: The little triangle makes the 7 redundant: CΔ is identical to CΔ7.

- The number **6** adds a major sixth to the major triad: C6 is C–E–G–A (R–3–5–6).

- All other **extensions** basically speak for themselves. A♭5 lowers the fifth (C–E–G♭); The C9 chord has an added minor seven and a high D; ♭9 turns this D into a D♭, and a ♯9 turns it into a D♯. Chords can be extended with 11s and 13s as well. A 9th chord consists of five pitches; 11th chords of six, and so on.

Accidentals first

Accidentals in chord symbols always refer to the following note. In C9♯11 the 11 is raised (F turns into F♯), not the 9.

> **The 7**
>
> *If you have a hard time finding minor or major sevenths on your instrument, you may use the following trick. For a minor seventh, you go an octave up, followed by a whole step down. A major seventh is an octave up and a half step down.*

TIP

No thirds

Not all chords are made up of stacked thirds. Some examples:

- There are various **suspended chords** or **sus chords**, including sus2 (1–2–5) and sus4 (1–4–5).

- **Cluster chords** are built up out of number of adjacent notes. On a keyboard instrument you can play such chords by simply pressing a number of adjacent keys.

INVERSIONS

Basically, you can play the pitches of a chord in any order you like.

- If the root note is the bottom note (the lowest pitch) of the chord, you're playing the chord in its **root position** (R–3–5, e.g., C–E–G).

- If you make the 3 the bottom note, you're playing the **first inversion**: 3–5–R (E–G–C).

159

- The **second inversion** has the 5 as its lowest pitch: 5–R–3 (G–C–E)

- Chords with four pitches have a maximum of **three inversions** (either the root or one of the three other pitches is the bottom note).

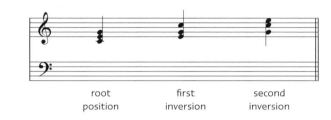

C major: root position and first and second inversions.

root position   first inversion   second inversion

Slightly different

Inverting a chord doesn't change its character. After all, you're still using the same notes that have the same mutual (interval) relations. The fact that the inversions in the example above still sound a bit different, is simply because the use a higher C (first inversion) and a higher C and E (second inversion) than the root position.

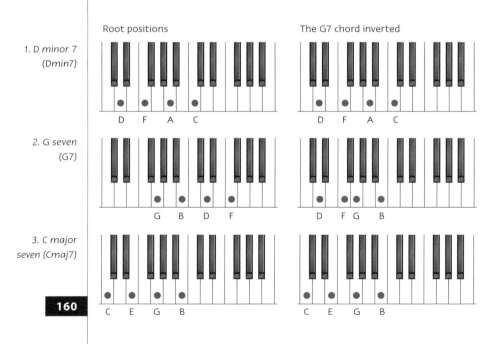

1. D minor 7 (Dmin7)

2. G seven (G7)

3. C major seven (Cmaj7)

Root positions   The G7 chord inverted

D F A C   D F A C

G B D F   D F G B

C E G B   C E G B

Easier

One of the main reasons to use inversions is that inverted chords make it a lot easier to go from one chord to the other, as the keyboard diagrams on the opposite page show you. If you play the three chords in the left column in their root positions, you have to move four fingers each time you go to the next chord. Inverting the second chord (G7), as shown in the right column, means that you have to move no more than two fingers when going from chord to chord — and it sounds better too.

Tipcode MOP-053

The same keys

As a general rule: If the next chord has one or more notes in common with the previous chord, play them on the same keys. The less you move, the easier it will be to go from chord to chord, and the better you will sound.

Notation

You're often free to play chords the way you want to (root position, first inversion, etc.), as long as you use the notes indicated by the chord symbol. If composers want you to play specific inversions, they have various ways to tell you:

• They can indicate the desired bottom note by adding a **slash and the new bass note** to the chord symbol: C7/E is the first inversion of the C7 chord, with the E as the bottom note.

• **A lower case b or a 1** after the chord symbol tells you to play the first inversion too; a lower case c or a 2 marks the second inversion, etc. An example: C7b is E–G–B♭–C (the first inversion has the second note as the bottom note).

Other instruments

Chord inversions can be played on all keyboard instruments and the harp, and on guitars as well: You can play the root note or any of the others notes as the bottom note, with the next note on the next higher string, and so on.

161

More variations

All of these instruments allow for many other ways to play chords as well. Page 155 shows you various spread voicings in 'Twinkle, Twinkle', for example. These 'wide chords' have the bottom note on the lower lines of the bass clef and the higher notes in the treble clef. Guitarists have infinite possibilities to play their chords higher and lower on the neck, with all kinds of different chord shapes. They often use all of their six strings to play three- or four note chords. As a result, some notes are played more than once: The E7 chord on page 166 has two Es and two Bs, for example. The same chord can also be played at the same position and with the same bass note, but with three Es and one B, again creating a slightly different sound and – possibly – an easier way to go to the next chord. The different ways to play chords are known as voicings.

Bassists

If the chord symbol indicates that the bottom note should not be the root note (e.g. C7/E), pianists invert the chord, as you have seen above. Bass players, who usually play the root notes of the chords in a piece, now play the new bottom note (the E, in this case).

Harmony

Using another note 'in the bass' makes for a slightly different sound, but it may also help to lead the music a certain way. A G7 chord, for example, tends to lead to a C chord. Changing the bottom note to a B (G7/B) makes this even more evident. This is an element of the subject of harmony (see pages 164–165).

Not all notes

Pianists, keyboard players and other musicians can leave out some of the notes of a chord. The fifth can often be skipped, for example. And if there's a bass player in the band, the keyboardist doesn't need to play the bottom notes of the chords per se; the bassist may even ask him or her not to. Composers sometimes tell you to leave out a certain note. If the chord symbol includes the term 'omit3', you need to leave out the third.

WHICH CHORDS?

If you want to add chords to a melody, you first need to know the key signature of the song. 'Twinkle, Twinkle' on page 154 is in C major. It only uses the white keys of that scale, so it seems only logical to pick chords that use those same white keys.

The first degree
Chords are built off of the notes of a scale. To see which cords you can make using the white keys of the scale of C major only, start at the first note or *degree* of that scale (C). Now play the first, the third and the fifth white key (1–3–5) and you'll hear the C major chord (C–E–G).

The second degree
Repeat this at the *second degree* of that scale (D): press the D with your thumb, skip one white key and play the third white key (F), skip one key and play the fifth white key (A). You are now playing a (D) minor chord, D–F–A.

The third degree, and so on
If you do the same at all consecutive degrees, each time playing the first, the third and the fifth white key, you'll end up with three major chords, three minor chords, and an augmented chord.

Three major chords
Because 'Twinkle, Twinkle' in C major, it makes sense to use the three major chords that you have found at degrees I, IV and V:

first degree	I	C major	C–E–G
fourth degree	IV	F major	F–A–C
fifth degree	V	G major	G–B–D

Note that those three chords contain all the notes of the C major scale.

Three minor chords
The chords on the second, third and sixth degrees of the scale are minor chords. These minor chords are often written in lower case Roman numerals.

second degree	II (ii)	D minor	D–F–A
third degree	III (iii)	E minor	E–G–B
sixth degree	VI (vi)	A minor	A–C–E

Primary and secondary chords
As you can see, chords I and III have two notes in common. The same goes for chords IV and II and for chords V and III. The major chords (I, IV, and V) are the *primary chords*; the minor chords (ii, iii, and vi) are their *secondary chords*. The secondary chords can replace their primary chords. In most cases, the primary chord will be replaced by the secondary chord that is a third higher (iii replaces I) or lower (vi replaces I).

TIP

Substitute chords
The 'replacement chords' referred to in the paragraph on primary and secondary chords are sometimes referred to as tonic substitute chords: They share a number of notes with the tonic chord, so they can be used with the same melody. There are different types of substitute chords, but they're typically chords that share two or more notes with the chord they replace.

HARMONY

Chords add color and character to the music, even to the simplest of songs — including 'Twinkle, Twinkle'. Take another look at the

164

music on page 155 while playing Tipcode MOP-059, and listen to the effect of the two different C chords in the first bar, or to the effect of the different chords under the four identical F notes in the third bar.

Secondary chords

The use of secondary chords is perfectly demonstrated in the same song, where the primary chord C in bar 1 is replaced by the secondary chord Am in bar 9 (note that melody is the same!), and the C/E chord in bar 2 is replaced by the secondary chord Em in bar 10 (again, the melody is the same). As you can clearly hear, these tonic substitute chords provide variety and add new colors to the music. (Note that both chords also have an added 7.)

And more

Chords do more than just that, however. They have a very defined role in any piece of music. Just like the leading note leads you to the tonic, for example, there are chords that lead you to the final chord of a piece. *Harmony* studies the effects of intervals, chords, chord progressions and all related subjects.

Dominant seventh chords

Here's an example: Adding a 7 to the chord on the fifth degree makes for a *dominant seventh chord*. In a piece in C major, this is the G7 chord.

V to I

This G7 chord (V) clearly leads to the root chord or *tonic* (I) of the piece, as is demonstrated in the chord progressions on page 160. If you play the corresponding Tipcode (MOP-053), you will clearly hear how the suspense or tension in G7 resolves in the I chord (C). The note B in the G chord plays an important role here. This can be stressed by turning it onto the bottom note (G7/B), as shown earlier in this chapter. Tipcode MOP-061 briefly demonstrates the effect.

Tipcode MOP-061

165

Set orders

You will find that many songs and compositions use set orders of chords, such as II - V - I (as in the example above), or I - V - IV, or I - IV - I. They are typically referred to as *chord progressions*.

The blues

One of the best known progressions that uses the chords I, IV and V is the blues, which perfectly shows the infinite musical possibilities that three basic chords allow for. The blues is a twelve bar form. The twelfth chord (E7, in the example below) is known as the *turnaround*: At that chord, you 'turn around' and start again at the first chord. If you want to end the song, you replace this chord by the tonic (A7, in this example).

The blues.

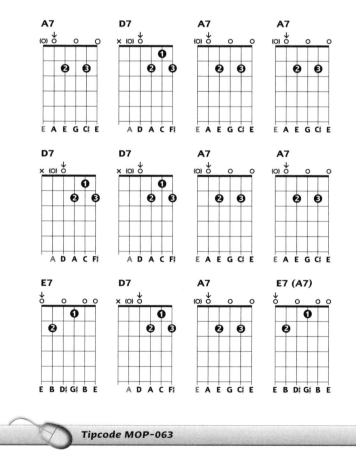

Tipcode MOP-063

TIPBOOK MUSIC ON PAPER

In numbers
Here's the same blues in numbers:

bars	chord degrees			
1 – 4	I	IV	I	I
5 – 8	IV	IV	I	I
9 – 12	V	IV	I	V (I)

Unexpected
Of course, composers and songwriters don't always choose
chords that logically follow on the preceding chords. By selecting
different, unexpected chords, they can create different songs,
songs that are intended to fascinate, surprise, or even shock the
listener, rather than easy-listening music.

19

Tabs, Chord Diagrams, Drum Notation

In addition to traditional music notation, there are various other ways to put music on paper. Here are some examples, including music notation for drums and percussion.

In previous chapters of this book you have seen several examples of keyboard diagrams with black dots indicating which keys to press for a specific note or chord (see page 160). Such diagrams aren't used to write music, but to demonstrate chords, chord inversions, and similar subjects. They can be found in books (e.g. *Tipbook Piano*, see page 230), online, or in small digital *chord finders* that present numerous chord diagrams at the push of a button or two.

Chord diagrams for guitarists

Similar *chord diagrams* are very popular among guitarists. These diagrams represent a section of the guitar fingerboard, displaying the actual *chord form* that you should play. Vertical lines represent the strings, and there are horizontal lines for the frets. Dots tell you where to put your fingers, and additional symbols may be used to indicate open or muted strings. The sounding pitches for each string may be shown too, as in the following example. If the chord form is to be played further up the neck, there will also be a number indicating how many frets up the neck your hand should be placed.

Play string 3 at the first fret with your index finger, play string 5 at the second fret with your middle finger, and play string 4 at the second fret with your ring finger. The result is an E-major chord.

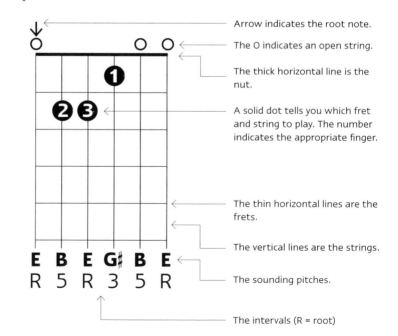

Arrow indicates the root note.

The O indicates an open string.

The thick horizontal line is the nut.

A solid dot tells you which fret and string to play. The number indicates the appropriate finger.

The thin horizontal lines are the frets.

The vertical lines are the strings.

The sounding pitches.

The intervals (R = root)

Books and apps

Chord diagrams for guitarists are easy to read and use as they reflect the exact 'shape' of the chord. They're primarily used to learn new chords and chord shapes. *Tipbook Acoustic Guitar* (page 227) and *Tipbook Electric Guitar* (page 228) offer hundreds of chord diagrams, including power chords, barre chords and movable chords, and there are dedicated chord diagram books as well. Alternatively, go online, get a digital chord finder (see above) or see if there's an app available for your smartphone.

Tabs

Chords can also be shown in so-called *tabs* (short for *tablature*). Tab notation is both easy and powerful—especially because it can show both the progression of chords and single-notes (e.g., solos) over time through the music.

Chord tabs

Tab notation uses numbers to indicate where to fret the strings. The first number or symbol refers to the low E-string, the second to the A-string, and so on. A '0' indicates an open string; an 'X' indicates strings that you should not play. This way, the D7 chords on page 166 are written as X–X–0–2–1–2.

Dashed lines

There are many websites that offer chord tabs for numerous popular songs (search for 'guitar tabs'). These tabs usually look like the ones below. The example below shows a brief chord progression that uses the same chords as the blues on page 166. The dashed horizontal lines represent the strings, usually going from high E to low E (top to bottom). This example lists the names of the strings as well; they're usually left out.

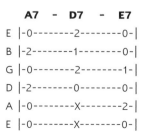

```
         A7   -   D7   -   E7
    E |-0--------2--------0-|
    B |-2--------1--------0-|
    G |-0--------2--------1-|
    D |-2--------0--------0-|
    A |-0--------X--------2-|
    E |-0--------X--------0-|
```

171

Solo tabs

Tabs can also be used for solos, melodies, or bass lines. They're similar to the tabs in the previous paragraph. The horizontal lines (the *tab staff*) represent the strings, and the numbers on the strings tell you at which frets you should stop them, just like the chord tabs on the previous page. The numbers below the staff tell which finger to use for each note. To complete the picture, the numbers of the strings may be indicated at the beginning of the staff, and the letters TAB may replace the traditional clef, as shown below. Tipcode MOP-054 plays the following bass line.

The tablature staff represents a guitar neck.

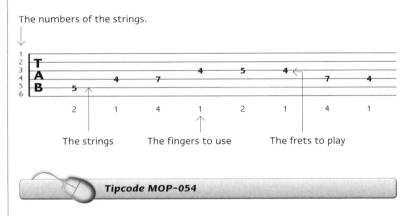

The numbers of the strings.

The strings   The fingers to use   The frets to play

Tipcode MOP-054

Standard notation included

Tablature doesn't show the exact duration of the notes of a melody or a bass line, or when to play them: The rhythm is suggested, rather than defined. That's why song books with tablature usually include standard notation too. If you know the song, you will usually be able to play the rhythm of the melody correctly, so you can rely on tabs only.

KLAVAR

Klavarskribo or *Klavar,* a notation system for pianists and other keyboard players, claims to be much easier to read than traditional notation. The system uses white (open) notes for the white keys, and black notes for the black keys.

Vertical staff

The vertical staff has twelve positions, one for each note in the octave. The notes indicate the corresponding keys. This eliminates the need for sharps and flats. The system doesn't need traditional rests either. Instead, a stop symbol indicates the note has to end, or notes simply sound until the following note starts. The stem of the notes points to the right or the left, indicating which hand to use.

Software

A considerable number of songs and compositions have been transcribed into Klavar, and there's special software available to convert traditional notation into the system. Klavar, an invention of Dutchman Cornelis Pot, was introduced in 1931.

DRUMS AND PERCUSSION

Most drums and percussion instruments — from bass drums and snare drums to cow bells and cymbals — do not produce an identifiable pitch. They're known as *unpitched instruments.* This is reflected in the *neutral clef* or *percussion clef* that is typically used for the parts for these instruments. It comes in two shapes, either a small rectangle or two vertical lines.

Neutral clefs
or percussion
clefs.

Drums

Charts for set drummers are typically printed on a regular five-line staff, the positions of the notes now indicating the components of the drum set. The snare drum notes are in the third space, while the lower sounding bass drum is in the first space. Cross-shaped noteheads indicate the cymbals. A similar note below the first line tells the drummer to depress the hi-hat pedal, closing the hi-hat

173

cymbals. A basic rock beat is shown below. The notes above the fifth line can be played either on the (closed) hi-hat or on the ride cymbal.

A basic rock beat.

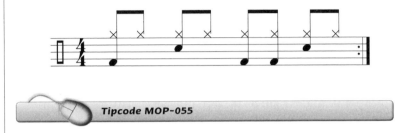

Tipcode MOP-055

Different notations

There is no standard notation for most of the other components of the drum set, and there are various ways to indicate special effects (such as rim shots, hitting the hoop and the drum head simultaneously) or additional cymbals and instruments (e.g., splash cymbals, crash cymbals, cow bells). Drum method books and drum magazines usually include a *drum legend* or *drum key* that summarizes the notation system used in that publication.

Drum legend as suggested by the Percussive Arts Society (www.pas.org).

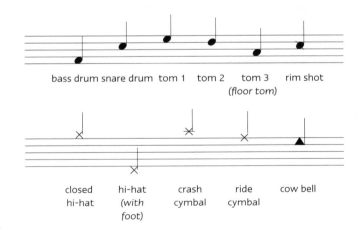

Less lines

Most drum rhythms or beats use the three main components of the drum set only: the bass drum, the snare drum, and the hi-hat or a ride cymbal. They are often printed on two- or three-line staffs.

Classical and marching percussion

Music for classical and marching percussionists typically uses a similar notation system. The music for a single instrument (bass drum or snare drum, for example) is often printed on a single line.

20

Putting Notes to Paper

If you can read music, you can also write it. Writing it down is easier than remembering it — whether it's a tune you just thought up, an idea for a solo, an exercise, or an entire symphony. Writing music is good practice too: Writing out scales, for example, is one of the most effective ways to really get to know and understand them.

The first section of this chapter deals with hand writing notes, but please take a minute to read it if you use your computer for music notation as well: You may miss a few helpful hints if you don't. Additional information on notation software is on pages 180–185.

Hand writing music

To put music on paper by hand, you need pre-printed music paper or *staff paper*, available in most music stores. You can also download a PDF with blank staff paper at www.tipbook.com or other websites. Free tab paper (see page 172), staff paper with pre-printed bar lines, and staff paper with treble and/or bass clefs is available online as well.

Pencils and fineliners

A pencil works well to jot down exercises or ideas, and it allows for easy corrections. Refillable lead pencils usually feature a built-in eraser. A fineliner or a pen should be used for the final version, especially if the sheet music needs to be photocopied or scanned.

- Drawing perfectly even noteheads takes a lot of practice and **a steady hand**. You may consider replacing the filled heads of quarter notes and shorter notes by simple slashes, as shown below.

Note heads are often drawn as slashes.

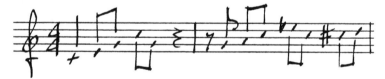

- In single-voice melodies **the stems** of the notes above the third (middle) line are at the left side of the note, pointing down. For notes lower down on the staff, the rule is reversed: The note stem is on the right side, pointing up.

- When writing **notes on the third line** (treble clef B; bass clef D), it usually depends on whether the melody is going up or down. If you use a beam to group a number of short notes above and below the third line, you can do as you please.

- If you print **two melodies** on one staff, write the lower one with all stems pointing down, and the other one with all stems

178

pointing up. Notes that sound simultaneously should of course be vertically aligned.

- If both instruments have have **the same note**, it gets two stems: one up, one down. If two notes are too close together to print one directly below the other, print one of the notes a bit to the right.

- In music for pianists and other musicians who read two staffs simultaneously, the staffs are connected by a brace (accolade). This *piano brace* turns the staffs into a **grand staff**. Take care to align the notes in the treble and bass staffs. Simultaneous notes in one staff use one stem.

The rhythm of each part should be correctly aligned.

- **Flags** are always drawn on the right side of the stem.
- Writing a correct quarter rest becomes easy if you think of it as a **tilted Z over a capital C**.
- Position **sharps and flats** so that they clearly indicate the heads of the notes to which they apply, as shown on page 46.
- There's no easy way to **draw a treble clef**. You'll just have to practice, or use staff paper with a pre-printed treble clef.
- **Use beams** if you divide a beat up into eighth or sixteenth notes. You may need to make an exception for vocalists, who usually want their notes to be lined up with their lyrics: Print a separate note for each syllable they sing.

179

- Reading music is easier if every bar has **the same length**. As a rule of thumb, you can divide every single staff into four equal bars. Pre-printed paper with bar lines is available online as well.

- Make sure you don't have bars **spilling over** to the next lines.

NOTATION SOFTWARE

Hand writing easily legible charts is not really easy. Notation software yields much better, cleaner results, and it allows you to immediately hear what you're writing.

Free or more
The most basic notation software can be found online. It is either freeware or it's very affordable, and experimenting with these programs is a great way to find out what this type of software is about, and to define your demands so you can make an informed purchase later on. These programs may have more options than you'd expect — but they may not allow for 'basic' things that you need, such as using an odd time signature. Spending some fifty to a hundred dollars buys you software that can do a lot more. Professional notation programs soon cost five hundred dollars or more. Note that some software companies allow you to upgrade their basic programs to more advanced editions.

Brand names
There are various companies that produce notation software, including Finale, GVox (Encore and MusicTime), Sibelius, and Geniesoft (Overture, Score Writer). Some of these and similar companies focus on either professional or affordable software; others do both, sometimes presenting a range that varies from high-end applications to ten-dollar entry-level programs.

The basics
Essentially, all notation programs work the same way. You select the time signature, the key signature, the number of bars of the

TIP

Audio production software

The programs mentioned above focus on music notation, all providing the option to play back the music you have written, using the instruments that you have indicated. Other programs focus on composing music and/or (digital) audio production, examples including Logic, Cubase, Cakewalk, and Notion. Such programs, also known as DAWs (digital audio workstations) or sequencing software, usually offer notation features as well, and a growing number of programs will bridge the traditional gap between true notation programs and audio production software. Tip: If you buy an audio interface or a dedicated audio sound card for your computer, audio production software is often included (a lite version of a professional program, in most cases).

composition, and the instruments you want to use. Printing notes is a matter of selecting the desired note value and clicking the correct position on the staff, which puts the desired note in place and produces the matching pitch, sounding the selected instrument.

Sharps, flats, etc.

The software automatically spaces the notes, which can be provided with accidentals, augmentation dots, ties, dynamic markings, ornamentation symbols, and so on. When you're done, you click the play button and the entire piece will be played back, using the instruments that you have selected. You can save the document just like you save a text or a digital photo, and you can of course choose to print or edit the document at a later date, to copy it to someone else, etc.

Entering notes

In addition to entering notes with your mouse, you can also use your computer keyboard (the letter C entering the note C) or a digital keyboard instrument such as a home keyboard or a digital piano: Playing the music will now automatically enter the notes.

181

Which keyboard

If you're using a home keyboard to enter the music, you can use the same instrument to play back all the parts you have created, from drums to violins and anything in between. If you want to use a keyboard solely to enter notes and play the virtual instruments that you have stored in your computer, all you need is a basic — and very affordable — controller keyboard. This type of keyboard has no built-in sounds. Just like any other digital keyboard instrument, you connect it to your computer using *MIDI*, the *Musical Instrument Digital Interface*.

Interface

MIDI basically is a set of agreements that allow for seamless communication between computers, home keyboards, synthesizers, and other digital (music) devices. Many of these instruments have special five-pin MIDI connectors, which you will also find on various audio interfaces for your computer (An audio interface basically converts your computer into a recording studio, usually allowing you to hook up digital instruments as well as electric guitars, microphones, etc.). A growing number of devices uses USB ports for MIDI instead.

TIP

Commands

MIDI, in a nutshell, is a system that uses all kinds of commands that tell computers or musical instruments what to do. There are commands that tell the device to play a certain note, which sound (which 'instrument') to use, how long to hold the note and at what volume to play it, and so on.

Scanners and microphones

Advanced notation software also allows you to scan printed charts, in a way similar to OCR (optical character recognition), converting the printed notes to digital notes. Some programs even allow acoustic musicians to enter notes using a microphone, the software converting the melody you play to the correct notes and note values.

Demos

Advanced and professional programs usually have more options and features than you will ever use — but low budget or intermediate software may not allow you to do everything you want. Luckily, most programs have free demos, so you can try them out and see what they can do before spending your money. Demo editions may not allow you to save or print your work (find out before spending a few hours entering your music!), or they print the word 'demo' all over the paper, for example.

Later years

Important tip: Many programs can save your music as a .musicxml file, the idea being that you can edit your work on a computer that runs a different program than the one you are using. Also, you don't lose all of your previous work if you decide to switch to a program from another company. As this doesn't always work perfectly, the best you can do is to invest time in finding the software that you can use for years to come. Ask around and find out which programs your friends or fellow musicians are using, and how they like them. Note that their responses may be confusing: While the majority seems to use the same word processing and photo editing software, there are many different opinions when it comes to notation software.

What they can do

A complete list of the features of an advanced or professional notation program would soon fill an entire chapter. Following are some basic features that give you an idea of what this type of software is generally capable of, providing a basic check list at the same time. This random list is also meant to inspire you to add your own questions and demands.

- Can you **enter notes** with your mouse, your computer keyboard, a keyboard instrument or a controller keyboard, a microphone, or a scanner, or can you import music from other programs?

- Does the software allow you to **add sharps, flats**, and other symbols later on?

- Can you add staccato dots and other markings to **a group of notes** simultaneously, or do you have to do this note by note?

183

- Does the program feature **all musical symbols** and markings that you need, including doits, scoops, inverted mordents, and other unusual symbols?

- Does the software support **chord diagrams**, chord symbols, and tabs?

- Do you have an unlimited choice of **time signatures**? Some basic programs do not allow for odd time signatures, for example.

- Do you get to hear the dynamic **effects**, ornamentations, articulation, and other effects that you have marked?

- Some programs feature **human playback** or a similar function that adds a human feel to the timing of the computer-generated notes.

- What's the maximum **number of staffs** for a composition?

- Can you **write multiple voices** on one staff (pages 178–179)?

- Does the program match the syllables of song **lyrics** to the corresponding notes? What is the maximum number of text lines? Can you change the font of the lyrics?

- Is the software capable of generating **tabs and chord diagrams**?

- Can you edit or choose the **shape of the note head** (e.g., cross-shaped noteheads)? Are various note fonts available? Some programs include a 'hand-written' font as well.

- Can this program play **MP3 files** or other digital audio formats? This is a helpful feature if you want to transcribe existing songs.

- Which **file formats** are available to save your music? MIDI allows you to play your music on other computers and a variety of digital instruments; MP3 and WAV files are audio formats; PDF makes for small, printable files; musicxml allows you to import your music into other notation programs; JPG and TIFF files turn your music into an illustration that can be imported into a text file, for example. Tip: Some programs use the same standard extension to save files, but that doesn't necessarily mean that files from program A can be read by or edited in program B or vice versa.

21

History

Music notation wasn't invented in one beat. Like most musical instruments, it evolved, step by step. This chapter takes a quick look at its history, from neums to notes, and from lines to staves.

Pythagoras is credited with creating the chromatic scale, which divides the octave into twelve equal steps, around 2,500 years ago. About a thousand years later these notes were given their letter names.

Written music

Some of the oldest surviving examples of written Western music are the Gregorian chants, named after Pope Gregory the Great (540–604). Little marks (neums) were added to the texts of these chants to indicate the direction of the melody.

Lines

Some four centuries later, a single line was used to indicate a particular pitch. The invention of the four-line staff, in the first half of the eleventh century, is attributed to the Italian monk Guido of Arezzo (c. 991– c. 1050). Modern notes and rests can already be recognized in manuscripts dating from that time. The five-line staff has been common since the thirteenth century, and musical notation has remained basically unchanged since the seventeenth century.

A four-line staff with Gregorian music.

Ut, re, mi

To make learning to read music a bit easier, Guido of Arezzo paired syllables with the various pitches, using the words from a hymn to Saint John. The result was the sequence Ut, Re, Mi, Fa, Sol, La.

Do, Re, Mi

Around 1600, a seventh note (Si) was added to this sequence, now covering the entire major scale: Ut, Re, Mi, Fa, Sol, La, Si, Ut, in which Si is short for Sancte Ioannes (Saint John). Later, Si became Ti, and the church changed the syllable Ut to Do, stating that God (*Do*minum) was the root — the beginning and the end — of all things.

188

The hymn to Saint John.

Italian

The Roman Catholic Church, ruled from the Vatican in Rome, has always had a lot of influence on music history. Over the centuries it issued all sorts of rules and guidelines, covering pretty much every aspect from notation to composition. This is one reason why you come across so many Italian words and abbreviations in sheet music.

Glossary

This glossary briefly explains most of the musical terms touched on in this book. It also contains some terms that haven't been mentioned yet, but which you may come across elsewhere. Most terms are explained in more detail as they are introduced in this book. For missing terms, please consult the index on pages 222–226 and the additional index on the inside of the front and back covers.

A tempo
Return to the previous tempo, after a quicker or a slower section. Not to be confused with tempo primo. See: *Tempo primo, tempo I°.*

Accelerando, Acc.
Get faster.

Accent
Stress a note, typically by making it sound slightly louder.

Acciaccatura
Ornamental note.

Accidentals
Sharps and flats that are not in the key signature, or natural signs.

Ad libitum
Literally: 'at liberty' or 'as you please'.

Adagio
Tempo mark. Slow; metronome marking 60–76.

Aeolian mode
Traditional mode, also known as A-mode. Similar to the minor scale. See: *Traditional modes and Minor, minor scale.*

Agitato
Agitated.

Al Coda
See: *Coda.*

Al Fine
To the end (a; = to; fine = end). Often used in combination with Da Capo (from the beginning).

Alla breve
Cut common time or $\frac{2}{2}$. Indicated with the symbol ₵.

Allargando
Literally: 'broadening out': get slower and a little louder.

Allegro, Allegretto, Allegrissimo
Tempo marks.

Altered notes
All lowered and raised notes are altered (natural) notes. Most altered notes are black notes (C♯/D♭, D♯/E♭, etc.). See: *Black notes.*

Alto clef
C clef, indicating Middle C on the third line. Also see: *Clef.*

Andante
Tempo mark.

Appoggiatura
Ornamental note.

Articulation markings
Markings that indicate how to 'pronounce' a note (long, short, bold, broad, and so on).

Assai
Literally: 'much' or 'quite.' Used in combination with other indications. See: *Tempo markings.*

Augmented interval
A major or perfect interval enlarged by a half step. C–F is a perfect fourth, C–F♯ is an augmented fourth. See: *Interval.*

B♭ instruments
See: *Transposing instruments.*

Backbeat
Term used especially in rock and pop music. The drummer hits the snare drum on the backbeat — usually the second and fourth beats in four-four.

Bar, bar line
Music is divided into bars or measures using vertical lines (bar lines) drawn on the staff.

Bass clef
Another name for the F clef. See also: *Clef.*

Beams
Replace flags; used to group eighth, sixteenth, and shorter notes that make up one beat.

Beats per minute
Often abbreviated to BPM. The number of beats per minute indicate the tempo of a piece. See: *Metronome marking.*

Black notes
The notes that you can play on the black keys on a keyboard instrument (C♯/D♭, D♯/E♭, F♯/G♭, G♯/A♭, A♯/B♭). See also: *White notes.*

Blues scale
The classic blues scale is made up of whole steps, half steps, and two intervals of a step and a half (a minor third).

BPM
See: *Beats per minute.*

Bridge
The bridge literally bridges two sections of a piece. Also used to indicate the B-section in an AABA form.

Capo
The beginning. See: *Da Capo* and *Al Fine.*

C clef
See: *Clef.*

Chord
Three or more notes played simultaneously.

Chromatic scale
Scale made up of twelve half steps.

Chromatic signs
See: *Sharp*, *Flat*, and *Natural sign.*

Church modes
See: *Traditional modes.*

Circle of fifths
A circle containing all major and relative minor scales, including the number of sharps or flats in each scale.

Clave
The rhythmic basis for many types of Latin American music.

Clef
Symbol that specifies the pitch of the notes on a particular line on a staff, and thus the pitches of the notes on all other lines and spaces. The two most common clefs are the G clef or treble clef and the F clef or bass clef. The C clef is a moveable clef. The

193

word clef stems from the Latin word clavis (key).

Coda
The 'tail' or the end of a piece. Also known as postlude or 'outro.'

Common time
Four-four time or 𝄴. See: *Four-four time* and *Time signature*.

Compound interval
Interval that is larger than an octave.

Con brio
With brilliance.

Con fuoco
With fire.

Con spirito
Spirited, with vigor.

Consonant
Literally: 'sounding (well) together.' Consonant intervals are divided up into perfect and imperfect consonants. See also: *Dissonant*.

Counting unit
The lower number in the time signature, which tells you which note value equals one beat. See: *Time signature*.

Crescendo
Get louder.

Crotchet
British term for quarter note or rest.

Cut common time
See: *Alla breve*.

Da Capo
Play again from the beginning (da = from; capo = beginning).

Dal Segno, D.S.
Literally: 'From the sign.' Return to the sign 𝄋 (segno) and play from there.

Decrescendo
Get softer.

Degree
See: *Step*.

Demisemiquaver
British term for thirty-second note or rest.

Diatonic scales
Diatonic scales consist of two half steps and five whole steps in a certain order. Major and minor are the best-known diatonic scales. See also: *Traditional modes*.

Diminished interval
A perfect interval that has been reduced by a half step.

Diminuendo
Get softer.

Dissonant
'Not sounding (well) together'. Intervals are divided in dissonant and consonant intervals. See also: *Consonant*.

Do Re Mi
Sequence of syllables, representing a (major) scale.

Doit
Ornament: a short upward bend of the note.

Dolce
Sweetly, lovely.

Dorian
Traditional mode, also known as D-mode. Diatonic scale.

Dot, dotted notes
A dot after a note (a dotted note) means that the note lasts one and a half times as long.

Double bar line
Double vertical line, one thin, one thick. Marks the end of a piece.

Double flat
Indicated by ♭♭. Lowers a note by two half steps. See: *Flat.*

Double-high C
See: *High C.*

Double sharp
Indicated by ✕. Raises a note by two half steps. See: *Sharp.*

Downbeat
See: *Natural accents.*

Duplet
Two notes played in the time of three beats or notes of the same value.

Dur
Another name for major. See: *Major scale.*

Du-wah
Ornament, mainly used by mouth harp and trumpet players.

Dynamic markings
Signs and abbreviations that show how loudly or softly a piece should be played.

E♭ instruments
See: *Transposing instruments.*

Enharmonic
Any pair of notes, intervals or scales that sound the same but have different names.

F clef
Alternative name for the bass clef. See: *Clef.*

Fall
Ornament.

Fermata
A note or rest of indefinite length. Also known as pause.

Fifth
Interval of five steps (e.g., C to G).

Fine
Finish, end. This is where it really stops. See: *Al Fine.*

First ending
The last bar of bars of a repeated section may be different the second (third, fourth, etc.) time around. If so, these bars are marked as first and second (etc.) endings, marked by a square bracket and the corresponding numbers.

Flat
1. Symbol (♭) indicating that a note must be lowered by one half step.

195

2. Too low. A guitar string that sounds flat should be tuned up.

Forte (*f*), fortissimo (*ff*), fortississimo (*fff*)
Loud, very loud, as loud as possible.

Forte-piano (*fp*)
Loud, followed immediately by soft.

Four-four time
Common time or ⁴₄.

Fourth
Interval of four steps (e.g., C to F).

G clef
Alternative name for treble clef. See: *Clef.*

Ghost note
Ornament. Smothered, 'dead' note.

Glissando
Ornament. Slide from one note to the next.

Grace note
Ornament: a 'small' note immediately preceding the main one.

Grupetto
See: *Turn.*

Gypsy scale
Scale with an interval of one-and-a-half steps in two places.

Hairpin
(De)crescendo wedge. See: *Crescendo* and *Decrescendo.*

Half step
A minor second; the smallest distance between two notes in Western

music (e.g., from C to C♯). Also referred to as half tone or semitone.

Half tone
See: *Half step.*

Harmonic minor
Alteration of the natural minor scale. Harmonic minor has a raised seventh step.

Hexatonic scale
See: *Whole tone scale.*

High C
High C typically refers to the C in the third space of the treble clef (C5, i.e., the fifth C on a piano keyboard, counting from the left). If a soprano sings high C, this usually refers to C6, which is also known as double-high C. The highest C on a piano is C8.

Home note
See: *Root.*

Imperfect consonant
See: *Consonant.*

Interlude
An interlude joins two different parts of a piece. See also: *Bridge.*

Interval
The distance from one note to another, including the first note. Intervals are divided into major and perfect intervals, and into consonant and dissonant intervals.

Inverted mordent
Short trill to the note above the main note.

Ionian
Traditional mode, also known as C-mode. Similar to the major scale. See: *Traditional modes* and *Major scale.*

Irregular time signature
See: *Odd time signature.*

Key
The key refers to the scale that a piece of music is based on. If a piece is in A major, it is based on the scale of A major.

Key note
See: *Root.*

Key signature
The sharp(s) or flat(s) at the beginning of a staff. The key signature tells you the key the piece is in, and which note(s) to raise or to lower.

Larghetto
A little less slow (metronome marking 60–66).

Largo
Very slow (metronome marking 40–60).

Leading note, leading tone
Note that leads to the root or home note. Also known as subtonic.

Ledger lines
Short lines drawn above and below the staff, used to extend its range.

Legato
'Bound'. When playing legato, each note flows into the next one.

Lento
Slow, dragging.

Lift
Ornament: slide up to the note.

Loco
Ends a section that's marked to be played one or two octaves higher or lower.

Locrian
Traditional mode, also known as B-mode. Diatonic scale. See: *Traditional modes.*

Lydian
Traditional mode, also known as F-mode. Diatonic scale. See: *Traditional modes.*

Major
1. See: *Major scale.* 2. See: *Interval.*

Major scale
Scale with whole (W) and half (H) steps in the following order: W W H W W W H. Similar to the Ionian mode. See: *Minor, minor scale.*

Marcato
'Marked'. The notes in a marcato passage must be given extra emphasis.

Measure
See: *Bar.*

Melodic minor
Alteration of the natural minor scale; the sixth and seventh steps are raised.

197

Meno
Less.

Meter
Measurement of time in music. The meter of a piece indicates the number of beats assigned to each measure or bar.

Metronome
Electronic or mechanical device that indicates the tempo with ticks, beeps, or flashes.

Metronome marking
Indicates how fast a piece must be played, expressed in the number of beats per minute (BPM).

Mezzo forte (*mf*)
Moderately loud.

Mezzo piano (*mp*)
Moderately soft.

Middle C
The C written on the first ledger line below the treble clef, and the first line above the bass clef. On a piano, Middle C is the C in the middle of the keyboard. Also known as C4: It is the fourth C on a piano keyboard, counting from the left.

Minim
British term for half note or rest.

Minor interval
Reduced major interval.

Minor, minor scale
Scale with whole (W) and half (H) steps in the following order: W H

W W H W W. Compared to a major scale, the third, sixth, and seventh steps are flattened (e.g., C D E♭ F G A♭ B♭ C). A minor chord has a flattened third (e.g., C, E♭, G).

Mixolydian
Traditional mode, also known as G-mode. Diatonic scale.

Modal music
Music that's based on the structure of a certain mode. See: *Mode*.

Mode
Scale (e.g., the traditional modes).

Moderato
Medium tempo: not too fast, not too slow (metronome marking 108-120).

Modulation
Change of key.

Moll
Another name for minor. See: *Minor, minor scale*.

Molto
Italian for 'very'.

Mordent
Short trill to the note below the main note.

Movable Do
The movable Do represents the root of a scale. See: *Do, Re, Mi*.

Natural accents
In ¼, beats 1 and (to a lesser extent) 3 are naturally accented. In ⅜, the first and fourth beats have a natural

accent. Also known as strong beats, (principal) metric accents, accented beats, or downbeats. The second and fourth beat in $\frac{4}{4}$ are known as the weak beats, unaccented beats, or upbeats.

Natural minor
The regular, unaltered minor scale, also known as original or pure minor. See: *Harmonic minor* and *Melodic minor*.

Natural sign
Sign indicating that a sharp or flat, either in the key signature or as an accidental within the music, must be (temporarily) cancelled: ♮

Naturals
The naturals or natural notes are the notes sounded by the white keys of a keyboard instrument. Also called white notes. See: *White notes*.

Non troppo
Italian for 'not too much.'

Note value
The duration of a note.

Octatonic scale
A scale made up of alternating half and whole steps.

Octave
Interval that spans eight white notes on a piano keyboard.

Odd time signature
Time signature in which each bar is made up of groups of two and three beats. (e.g., $\frac{5}{4}$, $\frac{7}{4}$, $\frac{10}{8}$)

Original minor
See: *Natural minor*.

Ornamentations
Various symbols used to indicate that a note should be embellished with extra notes or trills.

Outro
See: *Coda*.

Parallel
Keys with the same root are parallel keys, e.g., C major and C minor.

Pause
See: *Fermata*.

Pentatonic scales
Pentatonic scales are made up of five notes (penta = five).

Perfect consonant
See: *Consonant*.

Phrase mark
Curved line indicating that a group of notes should be played as a phrase.

Phrygian
Traditional mode, also known as E-mode. Diatonic scale.

Piano (p), pianissimo (pp), pianississimo, (ppp)
Soft, very soft, as soft as possible.

Pickup, pickup bar
An incomplete bar at the beginning of a piece or a musical phrase . Also known as upbeat.

Pitch bend
'Bending' the pitch of a note up or down.

Più
Italian for 'more'.

Pizzicato
If a violinist plays pizzicato, the strings are plucked, not bowed. See: *Articulation markings.*

Plop
Ornament. 'Falling into the note.'

Poco, poco a poco
Italian for 'a little,' 'gradually' or 'bit by bit.'

Portato
See: *Tenuto.*

Postlude
See: *Coda.*

Prestissimo
Very fast (metronome marking 200 or more).

Presto
Fast (metronome marking 176–200).

Quaver
British term for eighth note. A quaver rest is a quarter rest.

Quintuplet
A note divided into five equal parts.

Rallentando, rall.
Get slower.

Relative major, relative minor
Major and minor keys with the same key signature.

Reminder accidentals
Sharp, flat, or natural signs that remind you that an accidental indicated earlier still applies. See: *Accidentals.*

Rests
Moments of silence in music.

Ritardando, rit., ritard., ritenuto, riten.
Get slower.

Root, root note
Also known as tonic, home note, or key note. It's the first (and last) note of a scale. Most pieces end on the root of the key in which they are written.

Rubato
Free tempo. In parts marked rubato you can't tap along with your foot: There is no set tempo.

Scale
Series of at least five notes, arranged low to high. The key signature and the root of a piece tell you which major or minor scale it is based on.

Scoop
Ornament: Slight bend in the note, from the main note down and then back.

Score
Usually refers to a book of music containing the parts of all musicians in a piece.

Second
Interval of two steps (e.g., C to D).

Second ending
See: *First ending.*

Section line
Double vertical (bar) line that groups two or more bars into sections.

Section markings
Musical signposts that indicate the various parts of a piece.

Segno
The Segno symbol 𝄋 indicates that you must go to the coda. See: *Coda* and *Dal Segno*.

Semibreve
British term for whole note or rest.

Semiquaver
British term for sixteenth note or rest.

Semitone
See: *Half step*.

Septuplet
A note divided into seven equal parts.

Seventh
Interval of seven steps (e.g., C to B).

Sextuplet
A note divided into six equal parts.

Sforzando (*sf* or *sfz*)
Loud and then immediately soft. This symbol is often followed by a crescendo. See: *Crescendo*.

Sharp
1. Symbol (♯) indicating that a note must be raised by one half step.
2. Sharp also means 'too high in pitch,' as opposed to flat. See: *Flat*.

Simile
Keep playing the same way. Keep playing staccato notes, for example.

Sixth
Interval of six steps (e.g., C to A).

Slur
A curved line, indicating that a group of notes should be played legato. Not to be confused with a tie. See: *Tie*.

Staccato, staccatissimo
Short, very short.

Staff
The (five) horizontal lines used for the notation of music. Staffs can be enlarged using ledger lines. Sometimes spelled as stave.

Step
1. A certain note in a scale or mode. The second step or degree of a scale is the second note of that scale.
2. Another word for tone: A whole step equals a whole tone (e.g., C-D). See also: *Whole step*.

Straight eighths
Also known as even eighths. The 'opposite' of swing. See: *Swing*.

Stringendo, string.
'Urgently'. Get a bit faster and louder.

Subtonic
See: *Leading note, leading tone*.

Swing
The word 'swing' tells you to play the eighth notes in a way that's com-

monly known as a triplet feel, as opposed to playing them as regular straight eighths.

Tail
See: *Coda.*

Tempo markings
Tell you how fast a piece must be played. See: *Metronome marking.*

Tempo primo, tempo Iº
Return to the original tempo. See: *A Tempo.*

Tenor clef
C clef, indicating Middle C on the fourth line. See also: *Clef.*

Tenuto
Notes with a tenuto mark should sound for their full duration, without joining them together. The same mark is also referred to as portato (stately, solemn).

Tetrachord
The two halves of a diatonic scale.

Third
Interval of three steps (e.g., C to E).

Three-four time
A piece in three-four time has the equivalent of three quarter notes in every bar.

Tie
Curved line tying notes of the same pitch to each other.

Time signature
The time signature indicates the

counting unit (upper figure) and the number of beats or counts (lower figure) per bar.

Tone
1. Another word for step. See: *Step.*
2. Another word for timbre.

Tonic
1. Root; first note or step of a scale.
2. Chord built off the first degree of a scale.

Traditional modes
The seven modes or diatonic scales that can be played using the white notes on a keyboard, made up of five whole steps and two half steps. Also known as church modes.

Tranquillo
Calmly.

Transcribing
Writing out the music of a performance you hear.

Transposing
Changing the key of a piece of music.

Transposing instruments
A transposing instrument sounds another note than the one the player reads and fingers. A B♭-instrument sounds a B♭ when you finger a C.

Treble clef
Another name for the G clef. See: *Clef.*

Tremolo
Quick repetition of one note, or rapid alternation between two notes.

Trill
Ornament: the word 'trill' about says it all.

Triplet
A note divided into three equal parts.

Triplet feel
See: *Swing and Straight eighths.*

Tritone
Interval that spans three (tri) whole steps (tones).

Tuplets
Triplets, quintuplets, and duplets (etc.) are collectively known as tuplets.

Turn
Ornament: a turn around the note. Formally called a grupetto.

Unison
'One sound'. The smallest interval (e.g., C–C).

Upbeat
1. The opposite of a downbeat. See: *Natural accents.*
2. Another word for pickup or pickup bar. See: *Pickup, pickup bar.*

Vibrato
Slight, rapid pitch fluctuation.

Vivace
Lively.

Weak beats
The first and third beat in a four-four bar. See: *Natural accents.*

White notes
The notes that you can play on the white keys of a keyboard instrument. Also known as naturals (C D E F G A B etc.).

Whole note
Open-headed note without stem. Lasts four beats in ¼. Not to be confused with whole tone. See: *Whole step.*

Whole step
A major second, equaling two half steps (from C to D, or from G♯ to A♯, for instance). Also known as whole tone, which should not be confused with a whole note: a note that lasts four counts or beats in ¼.

Whole tone
See: *Whole step.*

Whole-tone scale
Scale made up entirely of whole step intervals. Also known as hexatonic scale.

Tipcode List

The Tipcodes in this book offer easy access to short movies, photo series, soundtracks, and other additional information at www. tipbook.com. For your convenience, the Tipcodes in this Tipbook have been listed below.

Tipcode	Subject	Chapter	Page
MOP-001	Twinkle, Twinkle on piano keys	2	8
MOP-002	Do Re Mi Fa Sol La Si Do on piano	2	9
MOP-003	C, F, and an octave on piano	2	10
MOP-004	Half steps and an octave on piano	2	11
MOP-005	Twinkle, Twinkle in notes	2	13
MOP-006	Notes and keys	2	15
MOP-007	Reading two clefs simultaneously	2	16
MOP-008	Chords	2	19
MOP-009	Quarter notes, eighth notes and a half note	3	22
MOP-010	Note values (whole note – sixteenth notes)	3	23
MOP-011	Dotted notes	3	31
MOP-012	Notes with ties	3	32
MOP-013	Triplets	3	33
MOP-014	Quarter note triplets	3	33
MOP-015	Sextuplet	3	34
MOP-016	Quintuplets and septuplets	3	35
MOP-017	Twinkle, Twinkle in F: B is too high	4	40
MOP-018	Twinkle, Twinkle with lowered B	4	41
MOP-019	Two sharps raise all Fs and Cs	4	46
MOP-020	Natural sign	4	47
MOP-021	G♯ and A♭: a different function	4	49
MOP-022	Twinkle, Twinkle in D with F and F♯	4	43
MOP-023	Reading ahead (crescendo)	5	53
MOP-024	Metronome settings (240/40)	6	56
MOP-025	Accents	7	64
MOP-026	Staccato	7	64
MOP-027	Legato	7	65
MOP-028	Phrase mark	7	65
MOP-029	Pizzicato on a cello	7	67

204

MOP-030	Various ornaments	8	**70**
MOP-031	Minor scale	10	**89**
MOP-032	F major with B and B♭	10	**92**
MOP-033	Scale of A minor	10	**96**
MOP-034	Major third and minor third	10	**97**
MOP-035	The basic intervals	12	**109**
MOP-036	Perfect intervals	12	**109**
MOP-037	Major intervallen	12	**109**
MOP-038	Perfect and major, perfect and minor	12	**112**
MOP-039	Tritone	12	**113**
MOP-040	Dissonant intervals	12	**114**
MOP-041	(Im)perfect consonant intervals	12	**114**
MOP-042	Tension and release	12	**114**
MOP-043	The leading note	13	**119**
MOP-044	Minor with and without leading note	13	**120**
MOP-045	Melodic minor	13	**120**
MOP-046	F major and D minor: the difference	13	**124**
MOP-047	Non-diatonic scales	14	**131**
MOP-048	A C on four saxophone voices	15	**135**
MOP-049	$\frac{6}{8}$: two times three	16	**143**
MOP-050	$\frac{5}{4}$ on drums	16	**144**
MOP-051	Straight eights and swing	16	**146**
MOP-052	Claves	16	**147**
MOP-053	Chord inversions	18	**161**
MOP-054	Tabs: a bass line	19	**172**
MOP-055	Basic rock beat	19	**174**
MOP-056	A=440 / A=442	–	**216**
MOP-057	Messa di voce	5	**54**
MOP-058	Broken chords	18	**154**
MOP-059	Twinkle, Twinkle with chords	18	**155**
MOP-060	Four chords	18	**157**
MOP-061	A different bass note	16	**165**
MOP-062	Syncopated notes	16	**142**
MOP-063	Blues in A	18	**166**

205

Essential Reference

The following pages include a variety of tips, tools, and tricks that are good to have at hand for immediate reference, including the major and minor scales written out on staffs, all (ascending) melodic and harmonic minor scales, a do-it-yourself scale wheel, scale and chord pointers, the circle of fifths, and various systems of naming specific notes and octaves.

Photcopy this page, cut the circles out, and assemble them.

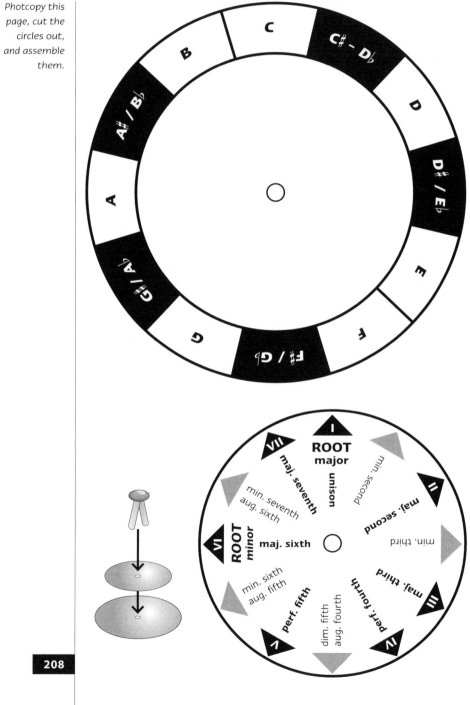

208

When photocopied and assembled, the scale wheel on the opposite page shows you the notes in each major and minor scale, and the names of the intervals within an octave.

Photocopy
Photocopy the two circles, glue them onto cardboard, cut them out and turn them into a scale wheel with a brass paper fastener as shown. The outer part is a one-octave keyboard, made into a circle.

Scales
If you want to find out the notes of a major scale, point 'ROOT MAJOR' at the root note of the scale. The black arrows will point to the notes of the scale. Use 'ROOT MINOR' for the minor scales.

Intervals
To find the name of an interval, simply point the 'ROOT MAJOR' arrow at the lower note; the abbreviated name of the interval will be at the upper note. Maj. stands for major; min. stands for minor; aug. stands for augmented; dim. stands for diminished.

CHORD POINTERS

The easiest way to figure out chords is to use the special chord pointers that you can download at www.tipbook.com. Print them out on thick paper or thin cardboard (check out the maximum paper weight your printer can handle!), punch a hole at the indicated position, and secure them together with a brass paper fastener as shown on the next page.

The first arrow
Now place the desired type of chord on your (piano) keyboard, the first arrow indicating the root note of the chord, and the chord pointer will point out which other keys to play. Check out the scale pointers on page 210 as well!

209

ALL MAJOR AND MINOR SCALES

The major and minor scales, printed on the following two pages, are the two most widely used scales in Western music.

Scale pointers

The scale pointers, pictured below, are a logical extension of the chord pointers that are shown above. Select the type of scale you want to play, and position the first arrow of the corresponding chord pointer at the first key of the scale on your (piano) keyboard. The chord pointer now indicates all keys of the scale. Download your chord pointers at www.tipbook.com and print them out on thick paper.

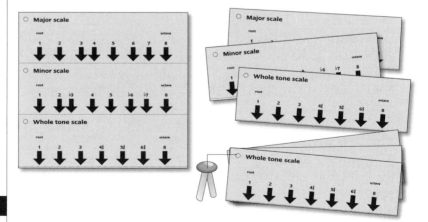

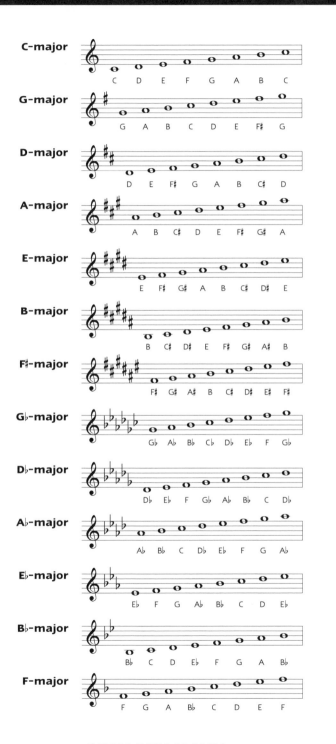

All major scales.

All minor scales.

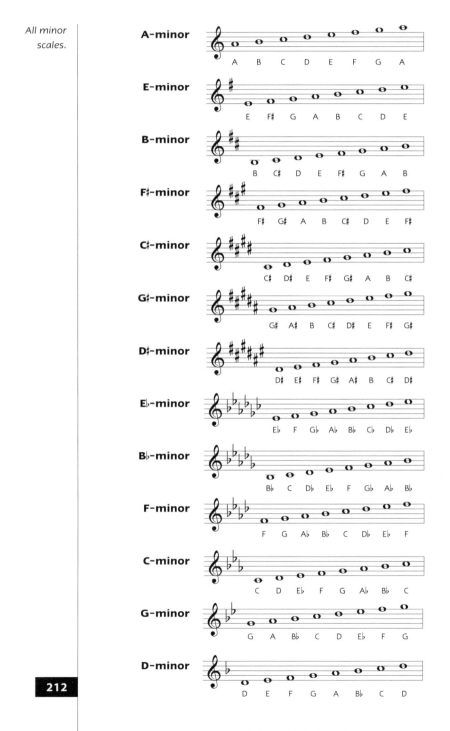

THE CIRCLE OF FIFTHS

You can read all about the circle of fifths in Chapters 11 and 13.

The circle of fifths with all major and minor keys.

KEY SIGNATURES

The fixed order of sharps and flats is covered in Chapter 10.

The sharps: F♯, C♯, G♯, D♯, A♯, E♯, B♯.
(**F**ather **C**harles **G**oes **D**own **A**nd **E**nds **B**attle)

The flats: B♭, E♭, A♭, D♭, G♭, C♭, F♭.
(**B**attle **E**nds **A**nd **D**own **G**oes **C**harles' **F**ather)

Use the mnemonic **G**o **D**own **A**nd **E**at **B**reakfast **F**irst to remember the number of sharps in the minor scales (G has one, D has two, etc.). Use the reverse order for the number of flats in those scales (F has one, etc.).

213

All sharps (treble and bass clef)

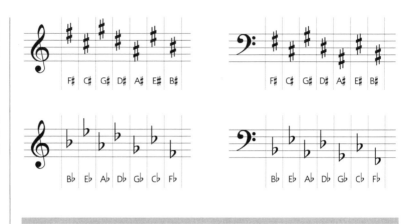

All flats (treble and bass clef)

THE OCTAVES

A piano keyboard encompasses a little more than seven octaves. Consequently, you can play a C on eight different keys, from low to high. To distinguish the various octaves and their keys, the octaves have been numbered. The first and lowest C on a piano, on the far left, is C1. The others notes in that octave are D1, E1, etc. The second C from the left is C2, and so on.

- Consequently, **Middle C** (in the middle of the piano keyboard) is C4.

- This makes the **highest C** (the very last key of the keyboard) C8.

- C5 (third space, treble staff) is often referred to as **high C**, and C6 as double-high C.

- Most bands and orchestras **tune** to the A in the fourth octave, i.e., A4 (see pages 215–216).

- The **three notes below C1** on a standard piano keyboard are A0, B♭0 and B0.

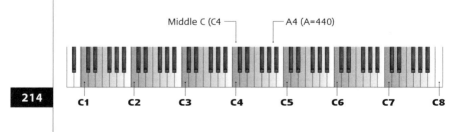

Middle C (C4) — A4 (A=440)

C1 C2 C3 C4 C5 C6 C7 C8

214

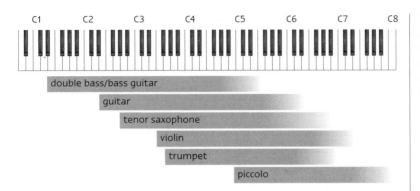

Other names

Occasionally, you may come across other systems of naming notes and octaves. Here are some examples.

US notation	Helmholtz pitch notation	Alternative notation	Key notation
C0–B0	C0–B0	CCCC	A0–B3
C1–B1	C1–B1	CCC	C4–B15
C2–B2	C–B	CC	C16–B27
C3–B3	c–b	C	C28–B39
C4–B4	c'–b' (c1–b1)	c	C40–B51
C5–B5	c"–b" (c2–b2)	c'	C52–B63
C6–B6	c"'–b"' (c3–b3)	c"	C64–B75
C7–B7	c""–b"" (c4–b4)	c"'	C76–B87
C8	c"" (or c5)	c""	C88

FREQUENCIES

Sound is vibrating air. If a guitarist plays the note A4 (first string, fifth position), that string vibrates 440 times per second. The speaker that reproduces this note also vibrates at that speed. Vibrations or cycles per second are stated in hertz or Hz.

• Most orchestras and groups tune to the note A4. The standard pitch for this note is 440Hz, typically indicated as A=440 hertz, A=440Hz or simply **A=440**.

215

- Some ensembles use a **slightly higher tuning** (e.g., A=442 or A=444) to make for a slightly brighter sound.

> **Tipcode MOP-056**

- The frequencies of **the lowest and highest notes** on a standard piano keyboard are 27.5Hz (A0) and 4224Hz (C8) respectively.

Harmonics

As that string vibrates at 440Hz, it also produces numerous higher frequencies, known as harmonics or overtones. The first harmonic equals the fundamental (440Hz, in this case). The second is at 880Hz: twice as fast, sounding one octave higher. The third harmonic is at 1320Hz, three times as fast — and so on, up to some twenty harmonics. The same happens if you play a wind instrument, for example. As you blow, the air column inside the instrument vibrates at the fundamental pitch of the note you play, as well as twice as fast, three times as fast, etc.

Character

The relative volumes of these overtones give a tone its character: They allow you to hear the difference between notes of the same pitch on a cello, a guitar, a saxophone or any other instrument. If you muffle the tone of an instrument (e.g., by using a mute on the strings of a violin), it sounds less bright because the mute reduces the higher overtones. Likewise, the du-wah effect described on

NOTE VALUES

American/International	British
whole note/rest	semibreve (rest)
half note/rest	minim (rest)
quarter note/rest	crotchet (rest)
eighth note/rest	quaver (rest)
sixteenth note/rest	semiquaver (rest)
thirty-second note/rest	demisemiquaver (rest)
sixty-fourth note/rest	hemidemisemiquaver (rest)

216

pages 67–68 influences the tone as you alter the harmonic content of the sound.

ONLINE SOURCES

The Internet is a rich source of information on the subject of this book, and you can find numerous (free) music lessons and musical exercises online. Below are some starting points; searching the Internet for the term "music theory" takes you to numerous other sites as well.

- Datadragon Music Education: datadragon.com/education/reading
- Free Ear Training On The Net: www.good-ear.com
- Music Theory Web: www.teoria.com
- MusicArrangers.com: www.musicarrangers.com
- Music, Composition and Theory, by Rowy: composer.rowy.net/index.html
- Music Theory Practice (Resources, tests ,and quizes) musictheorypractice.com/
- Ricci Adams' musictheory.net: www.musictheory.net
- Sightread This: www.sightreadthis.com
- Solomon's Music Resources: solomonsmusic.net
- Wikipedia, glossary: en.wikipedia.org/wiki/Glossary_of_musical_terminology
- Wikipedia, musical symbols: en.wikipedia.org/wiki/Modern_musical_symbols

Also check out Bart Noorman's Virtual Music School at virtual-musicschool.org.

CHORDS

Chord symbol	Alternative symbols	Pitches (C)
Major		
C	–	C, E, G
Csus4	–	C, F, G
C2	–	C, D, E, G
Csus2	–	C, D, G
C6	–	C, E, G, A
Cmaj7	CΔ	C, E, G, B
C6/9	–	C, E, G, A, D
Cmaj7^9	CΔ^9	C, E, G, B, D
C♭5	–	C, E, G♭
Caug	C+	C, E, G♯
C♯4	–	C, E, F♯, G
Cmaj7$^{\sharp5}$	C$\Delta^{\sharp5}$	C, E, G♯, B
Cmaj7$^{\flat5}$	C$\Delta^{\flat5}$	C, E, G♭, B
Cmaj7$^{\sharp11}$	C$\Delta^{\sharp11}$	C, E, G, B, F♯
Cmaj7$^{9\,\sharp11}$	C$\Delta^{9\,\sharp11}$	C, E, G, B, D, F♯
Cmaj7$^{\flat6}$	C$\Delta^{\flat6}$	C, E, G, A♭, B
Cmaj7$^{9\,\flat6}$	C$\Delta^{9\,\flat6}$	C, E, G, A♭, B, D
Cmaj7$^{9\,13}$	C$\Delta^{9\,13}$	C, E, G, B, D, A
Cmaj7$^{9\,\sharp11\,13}$	C$\Delta^{9\,\sharp11\,13}$	C, E, G, B, D, F♯, A
Minor		
Cmin	C–, Cm	C, E♭, G
Cmin2	C–2, Cm2	C, D, E♭, G
Cmin6	C–6, Cm6	C, E♭, G, A
Cmin7	C–7, Cm7	C, E♭, G, B♭
Cmin^{maj7}	C–^{maj7}, Cm^{maj7}, C–Δ, CmΔ	C, E♭, G, B
Cmin7$^{\flat5}$	C–7$^{\flat5}$, Cm7$^{\flat5}$, Cø	C, E♭, G♭, B♭
Cmin6/9	C–6^9, Cm6^9	C, E♭, G, A, D
Cmin7^9	C–7^9, Cm7^9	C, E♭, G, B♭, D
Cmin$^{maj7\,9}$	C–$^{maj7\,9}$, Cm$^{maj7\,9}$	C, E♭, G, B, D
Cmin7$^{9\,\flat5}$	C–7$^{9\,\flat5}$, Cm7$^{9\,\flat5}$	C, E♭, G♭, B♭, D
Cmin7$^{\flat6}$	C–7$^{\flat6}$, Cm7$^{\flat6}$	C, E♭, G, A♭, B♭
Cmin7$^{9\,\flat6}$	C–7$^{9\,\flat6}$, Cm7$^{9\,\flat6}$	C, E♭, G, A♭, B♭, D
Cmin7$^{\flat9\,11(omit3)}$	C–7$^{\flat9\,11(omit3)}$, Cm$^{\flat9\,11(omit3)}$	C, G, B♭, D♭, F, A

Steps (1 = R)	Full name
1, 3, 5	C major
1, 4, 5	C suspended (four)
1, 2, 3, 5	C two
1, 2, 5	C suspended (two)
1, 3, 5, 6	C six
1, 3, 5, 7	C major seven
1, 3, 5, 6, 9	C six nine
1, 3, 5, 7, 9	C major seven nine
1, 3, ♭5	C half-diminished
1, 3, ♯5	C augmented
1, 3, ♯4, 5	C sharp four
1, 3, ♯5, 7	C major seven sharp five
1, 3, ♭5, 7	C major seven flat five
1, 3, 5, 7, ♯11	C major seven sharp eleven
1, 3, 5, 7, 9, ♯11	C major seven nine sharp eleven
1, 3, 5, ♭6, 7	C major seven flat six
1, 3, 5, ♭6, 7, 9	C major seven nine flat six
1, 3, 5, 7, 9, 13	C major seven nine thirteen
1, 3, 5, 7, 9, ♯11, 13	C major seven nine sharp eleven thirteen
1, ♭3, 5	C minor
1, 2, ♭3, 5	C minor two
1, ♭3, 5, 6	C minor six
1, ♭3, 5, ♭7	C minor seven
1, ♭3, 5, 7	C minor/major seven
1, ♭3, ♭5, ♭7	C half-diminished
1, ♭3, 5, 6, 9	C minor six nine
1, ♭3, 5, ♭7, 9	C minor seven nine
1, ♭3, 5, 7, 9	C minor/major seven nine
1, ♭3, ♭5, ♭7, 9	C minor seven flat five
1, ♭3, 5, ♭6, ♭7	C minor seven flat six
1, ♭3, 5, ♭6, ♭7, 9	C minor seven nine flat six
1, 5, ♭7, ♭9, 11	C minor seven flat nine eleven omit three

Chord symbol	Alternative symbols	Pitches (C)
Dimished		
Cdim	C°	C, E♭, G♭, A
Cdim7	C°7	C, E♭, G♭, A, B
Dominant		
C7	–	C, E, G, B♭
C7sus4	C11	C, F, G, B♭
C7$^{♭5}$	–	C, E, G♭, B♭
C7^{9}	C9	C, E, G, B♭, D
C7$^{9\,sus4}$	–	C, F, G, B♭, D
C7$^{9\,♯5}$	–	C, E, G♯, B♭, D
C7$^{9\,♭6}$	–	C, E, G, A♭, B♭, D
C7$^{9♯11}$	–	C, E, G, B♭, D, F♯
C7$^{♭9}$	–	C, E, G, B♭, D♭
C7$^{♭5\,♭9}$	–	C, E, G♭, B♭, D♭
C7$^{♭9\,♯11}$	–	C, E, G, B♭, D♭, F♯
C7$^{♯9}$	–	C, E, G, B♭, D♯
C7$^{♯9\,♯11}$	–	C, E, G, B♭, D♯, F♯
C7$^{♯5\,♭9}$	C7alt	C, E, G♯, B♭, D♯
C7$^{♯5\,♭9\,♯11}$	C7alt	C, E, G♯, B♭, D♯, F♯
C7$^{9\,13}$	C13	C, E, G, B♭, D, A
C7$^{9\,♯11\,13}$	–	C, E, G, B♭, D, F♯, A
C7$^{♭9\,13}$	–	C, E, G, B♭, D♭, A
C7$^{♭9\,♯11\,13}$	–	C, E, G, B♭, D♭, F♯, A
C7$^{♯9\,♯11\,13}$	–	C, E, G, B♭, D♯, F♯, A
C7$^{♯9\,♯11\,♭13}$	C7alt	C, E, G, B♭, D♯, F♯, A♭
C7$^{sus4\,9\,13}$	–	C, E, F, B♭, D, A
C7$^{sus4\,♭9\,13}$	–	C, E, F, B♭, D♭, A

Steps (1 = R)	Full name
1, ♭3, ♭5, 6	C diminished
1, ♭3, ♭5, 6, 7	C diminished sevenC seven / C dominant seven
1, 3, 5, ♭7	C seven / C dominant seven
1, 4, 5, ♭7	C seven suspended four
1, 3, ♭5, ♭7	C seven flat five
1, 3, 5, ♭7, 9	C seven nine
1, 4, 5, ♭7, 9	C seven nine suspended four
1, 3, ♯5, ♭7, 9	C seven nine sharp five
1, 3, 5, ♭6, ♭7, 9	C seven nine flat six
1, 3, 5, ♭7, 9, ♯11	C seven nine sharp eleven
1, 3, 5, b7, b9	C seven flat nine
1, 3, ♭5, ♭7, ♭9	C seven flat five flat nine
1, 3, 5, ♭7, ♭9, ♯11	C seven flat nine sharp eleven
1, 3, 5, ♭7, ♯9	C seven sharp nine
1, 3, 5, ♭7, ♯9, ♯11	C seven sharp nine sharp eleven
1, 3, ♯5, ♭7, ♯9	C seven sharp five sharp nine
1, 3, ♯5, ♭7, ♯9, ♯11	C seven sharp five sharp nine sharp eleven
1, 3, 5, ♭7, 9, 13	C seven nine thirteen
1, 3, 5, ♭7, 9, ♯11, 13	C seven nine sharp eleven thirteen
1, 3, 5, ♭7, ♭9, 13	C seven flat nine thirteen
1, 3, 5, ♭7, ♭9, ♯11, 13	C seven flat nine sharp eleven thirteen
1, 3, 5, ♭7, ♯9, ♯11, 13	C seven sharp nine sharp eleven thirteen
1, 3, 5, ♭7, ♯9, ♯11, ♭13	C seven sharp nine sharp eleven flat thirteen
1, 3, 4, ♭7, 9, 13	C seven suspended four nine thirteen
1, 3, 4, ♭7, ♭9, 13	C seven suspended four flat nine thirteen

Index

Please check the glossary on pages 191–203 for additional definitions of the terms used in this book. As an additional index, most of the musical symbols used in this book are printed on the inside of the front and back covers.

225

226

The Tipbook Series

Did you like this Tipbook? There are also Tipbooks for your fellow band or orchestra members! The Tipbook Series features various books on musical instruments, including the singing voice, in addition to Tipbook Music on Paper, Tipbook Amplifiers and Effects, and Tipbook Music for Kids and Teens – a Guide for Parents.

Every Tipbook is a highly accessible and easy-to-read compilation of the knowledge and expertise of numerous musicians, teachers, technicians, and other experts, written for musicians of all ages, at all levels, and in any style of music. Please check www.tipbook.com for up to date information on the Tipbook Series!

All Tipbooks come with Tipcodes that offer additional information, sound files, and short movies at www.tipbook.com

Instrument Tipbooks

All instrument Tipbooks offer a wealth of highly accessible, yet well-founded information on one or more closely related instruments. The first chapters of each Tipbook explain the very basics of the instrument(s), explaining all the parts and what they do, describing what's involved in learning to play, and indicating typical instrument prices. The core chapters, addressing advanced players as well, turn you into an instant expert on the instrument. This knowledge allows you to make an informed purchase and get the most out of your instrument. Comprehensive chapters on maintenance, intonation, and tuning are also included, as well a brief section on the history, the family, and the production of the instrument.

Tipbook Acoustic Guitar – $14.95

Tipbook Acoustic Guitar explains all of the elements that allow you to recognize and judge a guitar's timbre, performance, and playability, focusing on both steel-string and nylon-string instruments. There are chapters covering the various types of strings and their characteristics, and there's plenty of helpful information on changing and cleaning strings, on tuning and maintenance, and even on the care of your fingernails.

Tipbook Amplifiers and Effects – $14.99

Whether you need a guitar amp, a sound system, a multi-effects unit for a bass guitar, or a keyboard amplifier, *Tipbook Amplifiers and Effects* helps you to make a good choice. Two chapters explain general features (controls, equalizers, speakers, MIDI, etc.) and figures (watts, ohms, impedance, etc.), and further chapters cover the specifics of guitar amps, bass amps, keyboard amps, acoustic amps, and sound systems. Effects and effect units are dealt with in detail, and there are also chapters on microphones and pickups, and cables and wireless systems.

Tipbook Cello – $14.95

Cellists can find everything they need to know about their instrument in *Tipbook Cello*. The book gives you tips on how to select an instrument and choose a bow, tells you all about the various types of strings and rosins, and gives you helpful tips on the maintenance and tuning of your instrument. Basic information on electric cellos is included as well!

Tipbook Clarinet – $14.99

Tipbook Clarinet sheds light on every element of this fascinating instrument. The knowledge presented in this guide makes trying out and selecting a clarinet much easier, and it turns you into an instant expert on offset and in-line trill keys, rounded or French-style keys, and all other aspects of the instrument. Special chapters are devoted to reeds (selecting, testing, and adjusting reeds), mouthpieces and ligatures, and maintenance.

Tipbook Electric Guitar and Bass Guitar – $14.95

Electric guitars and bass guitars come in many shapes and sizes. *Tipbook Electric Guitar and Bass Guitar* explains all of their features and characteristics, from neck profiles, frets, and types of wood to different types of pickups, tuning machines, and — of course — strings. Tuning and advanced do-it-yourself intonation techniques are included.

Tipbook Drums – $14.95

A drum is a drum is a drum? Not true — and *Tipbook Drums* tells you all the ins and outs of their differences, from the type of wood to the dimensions of the shell, the shape of the bearing edge, and the drum's hardware. Special chapters discuss selecting drum sticks, drum heads, and cymbals. Tuning and muffling, two techniques a drummer must master to make the instrument sound as good as it can, are covered in detail, providing step-by-step instructions.

Tipbook Flute and Piccolo – $14.99

Flute prices range from a few hundred to fifty thousand dollars and more. *Tipbook Flute and Piccolo* tells you how workmanship, materials, and other elements make for different instruments with vastly different prices, and teaches you how to find the instrument that best suits your or your child's needs. Open-hole or closed-hole keys, a B-foot or a C-foot, split-E or donut, inline or offset G? You'll be able to answer all these questions — and more — after reading this guide.

Tipbook Keyboard and Digital Piano – $14.99

Buying a home keyboard or a digital piano may find you confronted with numerous unfamiliar terms. *Tipbook Keyboard and Digital Piano* explains all of them in a very easy-to-read fashion — from hammer action and non-weighted keys to MIDI, layers and splits, arpeggiators and sequencers, expression pedals and multi-switches, and more, including special chapters on how to judge the instrument's sound, accompaniment systems, and the various types of connections these instruments offer.

Tipbook Music for Kids and Teens – a Guide for Parents – $14.99

How do you inspire children to play music? How do you inspire them to practice? What can you do to help them select an instrument, to reduce stage fright, or to practice effectively? What can you do to make practice fun? How do you reduce sound levels and

229

prevent hearing damage? These and many more questions are dealt with in *Tipbook Music for Kids and Teens – a Guide for Parents and Caregivers.* The book addresses all subjects related to the musical education of children from pre-birth to pre-adulthood.

Tipbook Music on Paper – $14.99

Tipbook Music on Paper – Basic Theory offers everything you need to read and understand the language of music. The book presumes no prior understanding of theory and begins with the basics, explaining standard notation, but moves on to advanced topics such as odd time signatures and transposing music in a fashion that makes things really easy to understand.

Tipbook Piano – $14.99

Choosing a piano becomes a lot easier with the knowledge provided in *Tipbook Piano*, which makes for a better understanding of this complex, expensive instrument without going into too much detail. How to judge and compare piano keyboards and pedals, the influence of the instrument's dimensions, different types of cabinets, how to judge an instrument's timbre, the difference between laminated and solid wood soundboards, accessories, hybrid and digital pianos, and why tuning and regulation are so important: Everything is covered in this handy guide.

Tipbook Saxophone – $14.95

At first glance, all alto saxophones look alike. And all tenor saxophones do too — yet they all play and sound different from each other. *Tipbook Saxophone* discusses the instrument in detail, explaining the key system and the use of additional keys, the different types of pads, corks, and springs, mouthpieces and how they influence timbre and playability, reeds (and how to select and adjust them) and much more. Fingering charts are also included!

230

Tipbook Trumpet and Trombone, Flugelhorn and Cornet – $14.99

The Tipbook on brass instruments focuses on the smaller horns listed in the title. It explains all of the jargon you come across when you're out to buy or rent an instrument, from bell material to the shape of the bore, the leadpipe, valves and valve slides, and all other elements of the horn. Mouthpieces, a crucial choice for the sound and playability of all brasswinds, are covered in a separate chapter.

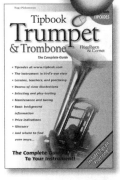

Tipbook Violin and Viola – $14.95

Tipbook Violin and Viola covers a wide range of subjects, ranging from an explanation of different types of tuning pegs, fine tuners, and tailpieces, to how body dimensions and the bridge may influence the instrument's timbre. Tips on trying out instruments and bows are included. Special chapters are devoted to the characteristics of different types of strings, bows, and rosins, allowing you to get the most out of your instrument.

Tipbook Vocals – The Singing Voice – $14.95

Tipbook Vocals –The Singing Voice helps you realize the full potential of your singing voice. The book, written in close collaboration with classical and non-classical singers and teachers, allows you to discover the world's most personal and precious instrument without reminding you of anatomy class. Topics include breathing and breath support, singing loudly without hurting your voice, singing in tune, the timbre of your voice, articulation, registers and ranges, memorizing lyrics, and more. The main purpose of the chapter on voice care is to prevent problems.

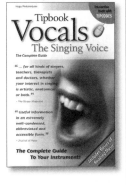

International editions

The Tipbook Series is also available in Spanish, French, German, Dutch, Italian, and Chinese. For more information, please visit us at www.tipbook.com.

231

Tipbook Series Music and Musical Instruments

Tipbook Acoustic Guitar
ISBN 978-1-4234-4275-2, HL00332373 — $14.95

Tipbook Amplifiers and Effects
ISBN 978-1-4234-6277-4, HL00332776 — $14.99

Tipbook Cello
ISBN 978-1-4234-5623-0, HL00331904 — $14.95

Tipbook Clarinet
ISBN 978-1-4234-6524-9, HL00332803 — $14.99

Tipbook Drums
ISBN 978-90-8767-102-0, HL00331474 — $14.95

Tipbook Electric Guitar and Bass Guitar
ISBN 978-1-4234-4274-5, HL00332372 — $14.95

Tipbook Flute and Piccolo
ISBN 978-1-4234-6525-6, HL00332804 — $14.99

Tipbook Home Keyboard and Digital Piano
ISBN 978-1-4234-4277-6, HL00332375 — $14.99

Tipbook Music for Kids and Teens
ISBN 978-1-4234-6526-3, HL00332805 — $14.99

Tipbook Music on Paper – Basic Theory
ISBN 978-1-4234-6529-4, HL00332807 — $14.99

Tipbook Piano
ISBN 978-1-4234-6278-1, HL00332777 — $14.99

Tipbook Saxophone
ISBN 978-90-8767-101-3, HL00331475 — $14.95

Tipbook Trumpet and Trombone, Flugelhorn and Cornet
ISBN 978-1-4234-6527-0, HL00332806 — $14.99

Tipbook Violin and Viola
ISBN 978-1-4234-4276-9, HL00332374 — $14.95

Tipbook Vocals – The Singing Voice
ISBN 978-1-4234-5622-3, HL00331949 — $14.95

Check www.tipbook.com for additional information!